Slave Law in the American South

LANDMARK LAW CASES
&
AMERICAN SOCIETY

Peter Charles Hoffer
N. E. H. Hull
Series Editors

MARK V. TUSHNET

Slave Law in the American South

State v. Mann in History and Literature

UNIVERSITY PRESS OF KANSAS

Published by the University Press of Kansas (Lawrence, Kansas 66049), which was
organized by the Kansas Board of Regents and is operated and funded by Emporia
State University, Fort Hays State University, Kansas State University, Pittsburg
State University, the University of Kansas, and Wichita State University

Library of Congress Cataloging-in-Publication Data

Tushnet, Mark V., 1945–
Slave Law in the American South: State v. Mann in history and
literature / Mark V. Tushnet.
p. cm. — (Landmark law cases & American society)
Includes bibliographical references and index.
ISBN 0-7006-1270-X (cloth : alk. paper) —
ISBN 0-7006-1271-8 (pbk. : alk. paper)
1. Slavery—Law and legislation—United States—History—19th century.
2. Mann, John, Chowan County, N.C.—Trials, litigation, etc. 3. Trials
(Assault and battery)—North Carolina—History—19th century. I. Title.
II. Series.
KF4545.S5T874 2003
342.73'087—dc21
2003006870

British Library Cataloguing in Publication Data is available.

Printed in the United States of America
10 9 8 7 6 5 4 3 2 1

The paper used in this publication meets the minimum requirements of the
American National Standard for Permanence of Paper for Printed Library
Materials Z39.48-1984.

TO EUGENE GENOVESE

CONTENTS

Although a labor system at its core and a set of social conventions in its everyday manifestations, antebellum Southern slavery could not have existed without the authority of law. Much of this law was statutory, developed over the long course of American experience with bound labor. Indeed, jurists of the period agreed that slavery existed only where domestic law established it.

The statutes of slavery varied from state to state but invariably defined slaves as the personal property, or chattel, of the master. But the rigor of statutory law existed in constant tension with an inescapable social fact: slaves were not things, like parlor furniture, nor domestic animals, like dray horses. Slaves were people, like their masters. They were people whom their masters knew well, sometimes from childhood. Individual slaves had personalities that masters routinely took into account in deploying slave labor. Although slave law gave to the masters almost total discretion to discipline slave laborers, social facts again dictated that negotiation and accommodation produced the best results from slaves.

Added to this inherent tension in the slave regime, the antebellum Southern master class was touched by the same romantic sentimentality and reformism as the rest of the country in the years before the Civil War. Moralistic sentimentality dictated that slaves be treated with sensitivity and basic fairness. Yet in these same years the profits to be derived from the internal slave trade, the need to bring more and more frontier lands under cotton cultivation, and the uncertainty of international markets for all southern staple crops demanded that slave law be imposed even more firmly.

When the rigor of the statutory law and the leniency of humane sentiments came into conflict, masters looked to the courts. Slave cases were not the most common items on dockets of Southern courts, but they were common enough for masters to seek coherent and consistent rulings on basic issues. *State v. Mann* (North Carolina, 1830) provided one such rule. Its subject matter was not particularly striking—a leaser using violent means to control misbehavior by a female slave—but its impact throughout the South at the beginning of a new era of proslavery thought and its impact throughout the North, particularly on the work of Harriet Beecher Stowe, makes *State v. Mann* a mirror of slave law at a crucial moment in its development. Meant—like its intellectual descendant, *Dred Scott v. Sanford* (1857)—to settle the law of slavery, it only showed how starkly that law contrasted with the ideals of free labor, equality, and democracy emerging in American law at the same time.

The author of the opinion in *State v. Mann* was Thomas Ruffin, one of the foremost Southern jurists of his day. He was a deeply moral and religious man and believed that good Christians must treat slaves with charity and decency. Yet for slavery to work as a labor system, a master's treatment of the slave must be free from the supervision of the state and the interference of those who thought slavery a wrong. Thus his opinion was as simple as the case itself: the power of the master over the slave must be absolute, and the law must allow no exceptions to the rule.

Georgetown law professor and historian Mark Tushnet is one of the foremost living authorities on *State v. Mann*, slave law in general, and the civil rights movement. To this book he has brought the insight of the teacher of law and the sympathy of the historian. He has rendered a complex subject clear and plain, and at the same time teased out from it all its ambiguities and ironies. Perhaps equally important, he has traced the impact of the case on the nascent abolitionist movement and followed it into the work of one of the most widely read of those critics of slavery— the novelist Harriet Beecher Stowe. In Stowe's work, Ruffin and his views appear in somber guise, the absolutism of the decision turning upon itself to warn of the coming trial of slavery by fire. Compact, deeply troubling, and intellectually vibrant, Tushnet's account reminds all of us how simple law cases can have great political consequences.

Introduction

State v. Mann, decided by the North Carolina Supreme Court in 1830, quickly became one of the most notorious American cases involving slavery. Abolitionist publicists execrated the decision as a demonstration that even humane Southern lawyers found themselves compelled to defend positions that they acknowledged were horrendous. Scholars have taken *State v. Mann* to express "the logic of slavery," as Eugene Genovese puts it in his comment on the case.

Mann's holding is easy to describe: Slaveowners cannot be prosecuted for assaults on their slaves. Its rationale was that slavery required for its maintenance that slaves be aware that they were subject to their owners' complete and total control and that they had no place to appeal when they believed their owners had abused them: "The power of the master must be absolute to render the submission of the slave perfect." For Genovese, "no civilized community could live with such a view."

Many landmark cases are important because of their consequences for society. *Mann* became famous, though, probably less for its holding, or even for the starkness of its rationale, than for the rhetoric with which Judge Thomas Ruffin, the opinion's author, framed his discussion. The opinion's first sentence reads: "A Judge cannot but lament when such cases as the present are brought into judgment." Judge Ruffin then referred to "[t]he struggle . . . in the Judge's own breast between the feelings of the man and the duty of the magistrate." After stating the opinion's rationale, Judge Ruffin wrote, "I most freely confess my sense of the harshness of this proposition" and asserted that "as a principle of moral right every person in his retirement must repudiate it." The opinion's final paragraph begins, "I repeat that I would gladly have avoided this ungrateful question."

State v. Mann's importance as a rhetorical performance was confirmed when Harriett Beecher Stowe made the case central in her second antislavery novel, itself of course a rhetorical performance. In 1853, Stowe published *A Key to Uncle Tom's Cabin*, in which she compiled evidence supporting the portrait of slavery she had painted in her famous novel. Early in *A Key*, Stowe insisted that she had tried "to separate carefully, as far as possible, the system from the men," creating characters to give the "fairest picture of our Southern brother." Judge Ruffin was an object lesson for her. He was among the "men of honor, men of humanity, men of kindest and gentlest feelings" who were "*obliged* to interpret these severe laws with inflexible severity." She quoted extensively from Judge Ruffin's opinion because his "remarks . . . are so characteristic, and so strongly express the conflict between the feelings of the humane judge and the logical necessity of a strict interpreter of slave-law." She "admire[d] the unflinching calmness with which a man, evidently possessed of honorable and human intentions, walks through the most extreme and terrible results and conclusions, in obedience to the laws of legal truth."

> No one can read this decision, so fine and clear in its expression, so dignified and solemn in its earnestness, and so dreadful in its results, without feeling at once deep respect for the man and horror for the system. The man, judging him from this short specimen, which is all the author knows, has one of that high order of minds, which looks straight through all verbiage and sophistry to the heart of every subject which it encounters. He has, too, that noble scorn of dissimulation, that straightforward determination not to call a bad thing by a good name, even when most popular and reputable and legal, which it is to be wished could be more frequently seen. . . . [T]here is but one sole regret; and that is that such a man, with such a mind, should have been merely an *expositor*, and not *reformer* of law.

For Stowe, *Mann* illustrated "cool legal humanity." It posed a challenge that she took up in *Dred: A Tale of the Great Dismal Swamp*, which she published in book form in 1858. *Dred* "has become a missing text in Stowe's canon," according to one scholar, but it reveals a great deal about her thought—and, through her, about abolitionist thought—regarding slavery, law, religion, and rebellion. As framed in the novel, *Mann* provides the occasion for a young lawyer to reflect deeply upon the possibilities of reform—and so, in a peculiar, backhanded way, *Mann* became a vehicle for reform.

Also in 1853, William Goodell, a New York abolitionist, publisher, and minister who helped found the abolitionist Liberty Party, published his overview, *The American Slave Code in Theory and Practice*. Judge Ruffin's opinion in *Mann* was the object of comment throughout the book. Responding to Judge Ruffin's observation that "[t]he end of slavery is the profit of the master," Goodell observed, "This honest judicial decision should shame the pretense that slaves are held for their own benefit." Later, in his extensive—and, as we will see, somewhat misleading—discussion of the punishment of slaves by masters, Goodell said of Judge Ruffin's opinion, "Here is a document that will repay profound study. The moral wrong of slavery is distinctly and repeatedly admitted, along with the most resolute determination to support it, *by not allowing the rights of the master to come under judicial investigation.*" Goodell saw the rule stated in *Mann* as betraying "consciousness that [the masters' rights] would not abide the test of the first principles of legal science." For Goodell, Judge Ruffin's description of the "struggle between the *man* and the *magistrate*" implied that "slavery requires of its magistrates to trample upon their own manhood," and "the cool and deliberate decision to do this" was a "painful and instructive [feature] of the exhibition." Notably, Goodell found Judge Ruffin's argument "impregnable," presumably because it exposed the necessary immorality of slavery and the law required to support it.

Perhaps even the South did not have to "live with" *Mann*'s logic, at least as abolitionist publicists understood the case. *Mann*'s holding was girdled with qualifications, some implicit and some explicit. Judge Ruffin's opinion ended by noting that the legislature could change the rule and make masters liable criminally for assaults on their own slaves. Genovese says that this expressed Judge Ruffin's hope "that the legislature would find a way to remove the high court's dilemma." Yet the suggestion that the legislature could change the law in a more humane direction also hints that Judge Ruffin did not think that the common law rule he applied—or created—was necessary for slavery's maintenance. After *Mann*, Southern lawyers—and the North Carolina Supreme Court itself—agreed that slaveowners could be prosecuted for *murdering* their slaves. Everyone agreed that strangers could be prosecuted for assaulting someone else's slaves. *Mann* itself actually involved a defendant who had hired the slave he assaulted, and Judge Ruffin said that the defendant might well be liable to the slaveowner for any damages his assault caused.

State v. Mann turns out to be more interesting than its portrayal by abolitionist publicists. Close examination shows how the case intersects with a large number of scholarly perspectives on slavery: the role of self-interest in slavery, the place honor held in the moral code of the Southern master class, the tension— whether real to Southern slave owners or only to modern scholars—between morality and the law of slavery, and more. The "logic of slavery" that Judge Ruffin exposed incorporated absolute *legal* dominion of the master over the slave, but *Mann* asserted that slavery could tolerate, and even demanded, constraints on the master's power through institutions other than law—what Judge Ruffin referred to as "the frowns and deep execrations of the community upon the barbarian who is guilty of excessive and brutal cruelty to his unprotected slave." Among these institutions were the South's churches. Abolitionist publicists derided the effectiveness of these institutions even as they insisted, with Stowe, on the power of moral reform through religion. And Southern preachers themselves were unsure that moral instruction would be sufficient, ordinarily referring to the law as a supplement, secondary but necessary, to moral instruction. Examined in detail, *State v. Mann* does expose the logic of slavery, but that logic was more complicated than Stowe and Goodell thought it was.

Chapter 1 introduces readers to the ways in which law shaped, and was shaped by, slavery. Chapters 2 and 3 offer detailed analyses of Judge Ruffin's opinion in *State v. Mann*. After summarizing the opinion, Chapter 2 explores the relation the opinion describes between law and other means of controlling masters' power, comparing that description to the one offered by abolitionist writers. Chapter 3 uses *State v. Mann* to illustrate the argument, developed by Genovese and critically elaborated by later scholars, that law was a means of maintaining the ideological hegemony of the Southern master class.

Shifting from the preceding chapters' close focus on the *Mann* opinion, Chapter 4 turns to the case's social setting. It provides a lesson in the limits to historical inquiry. Little can be known about the circumstances that gave rise to the case, but what little there is suggests rather strongly that the case was not a major one until Judge Ruffin chose to make it the vehicle for his reflections on the logic of slavery. The chapter then uses Judge Ruffin's biography to examine *why* he made that choice.

Chapters 5 and 6 take up Stowe's novel *Dred*, to show how she used *State v. Mann* to advance her ideas about the relation between law and moral reform—the idea, that is, that law is unrelated to, and might even obstruct, moral reform. Chapter 5 discusses *Dred*, and Chapter 6 turns to the views of *Dred* taken by literary scholars, and—because Stowe's novel addresses the question of whether it is possible to reform slavery—to some historians' analysis of the abolitionist movement.

CHAPTER I

Slavery and the Law

Slavery was a social system, an economic system, and a legal system. As a social system, slavery involved what historical sociologist Orlando Patterson calls "social death," the complete rejection of slaves, from birth to death, from the community of slaveowners. As an economic system, slavery involved slave masters' using the human beings they owned to produce goods that the masters owned, for whatever compensation the slaveowners thought appropriate (rather than, as in wage labor, for a compensation negotiated—although sometimes under conditions of inequality—between employers and workers).

The law of slavery supported the social and economic systems of slavery. Owning a slave was, after all, a form of ownership, itself a legal category. Implementing a comprehensive system of slavery required other laws as well: laws dealing with what could be done when a slave ran away from his or her owner, laws dealing with whether a slave's seller should pay damages to a new owner if the slave ran away, laws dealing with whether a slave's owner should pay damages if a slave burnt down someone's barn. Southern states developed the law of slavery through acts by their legislatures and through decisions by their courts. Understanding *State v. Mann* requires some exploration of the prior development of the law of slavery and of the different roles legislatures and courts played in that development.

The Origins of the Law of Slavery

A substantial scholarly controversy exists on the seemingly simple question, When did slavery come to the American colonies? Everyone agrees that slavery existed by the end of the seventeenth century. How it came into existence is a more difficult question. The problem is that at some point a relation of substantial domination and exploitation turned into a relation of owner and slave, but no one can identify when—or even how—that happened. Historians are unable to provide an answer because the available legal materials are simply too thin. The question asks for something precise, but the colonists who constructed slavery and the law of slavery were fumbling around to figure out the right way to think about something that was new to their practical and legal experience.

The resources for developing the law of slavery fell into two categories: the law of England, referred to as the common law, and Roman law and its successors in Europe, referred to as civil law (a term that in this context has a meaning quite different from the one it has when we talk about criminal law and civil law). Ordinarily lawyers used Roman law or the common law as a source of insight into the problems they faced, drawing solutions directly from earlier choices or finding the earlier problem similar enough to the current one to be a good source of a solution by analogy and minor adaptation.

Roman law might have been a good source for a law of slavery, because slavery existed in Rome and was supported by an elaborate body of law. Yet the Roman and civil law traditions were foreign to the Englishmen who were trying to work out the right way for their law to treat slavery. Early decisions made almost no reference to Roman and civil law, and there is little evidence that Roman and civil law influenced early conceptualizations of slavery, although by the time slavery ended proslavery legal thinkers relied extensively on Roman and civil law analogies.

There was a parallel difficulty in English common law: Slavery did not exist in seventeenth- and eighteenth-century England.

Medieval England's system of feudal law did have a status called villeinage. By the time the English colonized the South, there were no villeins left in England, but the legal ideas could be dredged up from old texts. Villeins were serfs, essentially farmers on lands owned by a lord, who was entitled to direct their labor however he wanted. But the contrast between villeinage and slavery as it developed in the American South was important. A villein was subject to his lord's command but legally was a free person in relation to everyone else. A villein might not have had a lot of actual liberty, but the mere fact that villeins had some freedom under the law meant that the legal concepts associated with villeinage could not be deployed in thinking about slaves, who had no freedom at all.

There was an additional complication. Neither Roman law nor the law of medieval England took account of the most obviously important characteristic of slavery in the American South: Slavery was a racial phenomenon. After a very short period in which legal thinkers struggled over whether whites and Native Americans could be enslaved, by the middle or (at the latest) end of the seventeenth century, Southern law settled on the position that slavery was a legal status confined to people of African ancestry. (Controversy persisted over *how much* African ancestry was essential for treating a person as a slave to be lawful, but *some* such ancestry was required.)

In a manner that legal historians still do not completely understand, racial slavery entered into the law of colonial America. Saying that the law recognized slavery says nothing about what the content of the law of slavery was.

———

Developing the Law of Slavery

Lawyers and judges facing new problems decide what to do by consulting "the law." Often that seems fairly easy. Some of the law can be found in the statutes that legislatures enact. Resolving the new problem means looking up the statute and applying it to the problem. Of course, sometimes the statute does not explicitly deal with the new problem (if it did, the problem would not truly be a *new* one). Lawyers and judges then interpret the statute, determining what it means in the case they are dealing with. We have several ways of describing what judges do when they interpret a statute: Sometimes we say that judges try to figure out what the legislature intended; sometimes we say that they try to identify the statute's purposes. No matter what the description, interpreting statutes requires judges to bring to the statute some background understanding of what the statute is about.

For example, Southern judges faced cases in which slaves were charged with murder, which in some states was defined in a general statute. The defendant slave (or perhaps more precisely, the lawyer hired by the slave's owner) might argue that the slave did in fact kill the victim, but did so in self-defense after the victim attacked the slave. The prosecution might reply that although self-defense was a defense in cases where the defendant was white, the case of a slave charged with killing a free white person was different because maintaining slavery required that slaves put up with assaults from whites and complain, if at all, to their owners afterward. The general murder statute might not say anything about the application of self-defense in cases involving slaves charged with killing free whites. A judge asked to instruct the jury on self-defense would have to think about the implications of the existence of slavery in interpreting the general murder statute.

The English common law tradition locates the law not simply in statutes but in judicial decisions as well. Murder, in fact, was traditionally a common law offense, meaning that courts *created* the offense and defined its boundaries without any input from a legislature. While slavery existed in the United States, the common law covered far more territory than statutes did. The law of accidents (torts, in lawyers' terms) and the law of contracts were almost entirely the product of the common law, not legislation. So was the law of property, including, of course, the property aspects of the law of slavery.

Judges deciding common law cases examined the precedents to find out what "the law" was. As with statutes, though, the precedents had to be interpreted in light of the judges' views of some background features of the legal and social systems. *Somerset v. Stewart* (1772) was probably the most celebrated eighteenth-century case about slavery, and it provides a good example of the common law reasoning process. *Somerset* involved a suit by a person who was held as a slave in Virginia. His owner brought him to England in 1769, expecting that Somerset would continue to serve him. Instead, Somerset escaped from his master. He was caught and locked up on a ship, awaiting departure to Jamaica. Somerset managed to get his case before a court, claiming that holding him as a slave was against the law. The case came before one of England's greatest judges, Lord Mansfield, who ordered that Somerset be released from the ship and allowed to live as a free person. Mansfield had no statute to rely on here. Instead, he rested his decision on general principles that, he said, were the underpinnings of the common law. According to Mansfield, the entire common law rested on a presumption of liberty. In Mansfield's words, "the state of slavery is of such a nature, that it is incapable of being introduced on any reasons, moral or political, but only by positive law." Slavery was "so odious, that nothing can be suffered to support it, but positive law." By "positive law" Mansfield meant statutory law. In the absence of a statute, the general principles of the common law meant that slavery could not exist. The precise holding of *Somerset* may have been quite limited, as Mansfield indicated in later decisions. Its rhetoric, though, was more expansive, and it was the rhetoric rather than the holding that became celebrated.

Somerset's case was widely known in the American South, which of course rejected the proposition that slavery was inconsistent with the common law. Accepting that proposition would have meant approaching every common law case involving slaves—contract cases, accident cases, and property cases—with a presumption that the law should be developed in ways that promoted the liberty of those held as slaves. A similar presumption would apply when courts had to interpret statutes. Somerset's case would have converted the law of slavery into a law of freedom.

Somerset's case, though, remains a good model for the common law decision-making process. Lord Mansfield had to decide Somerset's case guided only by his interpretation of existing common law as expressed in cases the courts had already decided. Yet, because the problem presented to him was a new one, he had to determine what principles justified the prior cases and then apply those principles to Somerset's case. The same process occurred in the American South as judges developed a law of slavery. Statutes—the positive law Lord Mansfield required—established the existence of slavery and defined its broad contours. Judges worked out the details of the law of slavery by identifying the principles they believed could make slavery into a coherent system of law.

––––––

The Law of Slavery in the
Early Republic (1789–1820)

Discomfort over the persistence of slavery pervaded the creation of the United States. It is hard to read the Declaration of Independence's statements that "all Men are created equal," that all men had inalienable rights, including a right to liberty, and that governments derive "their just Powers from the Consent of the Governed" without thinking that slavery was inconsistent with the principles for which the American Revolution had been fought.

Sentiment against slavery was in fact widespread as the nation's new Constitution was drafted in 1787. The drafters of the Constitution, meeting in Philadelphia, discovered that they would be unable to secure the Constitution's ratification if they allowed the Constitution to cast doubt on slavery. They avoided using the words *slavery* or *slaves* in the Constitution, but they included several provisions that recognized and even protected the institution where it existed. Congress was given the power to regulate commerce among the states, for example, but it was barred for twenty years from using that power to ban the "Migration or Importation of such Persons as any of the States now existing shall think proper"—one of the Constitution's euphemisms for "slaves." Representation in the House of Representatives was allocated according to the notorious three-fifths clause, saying that the population base for figuring out how many representatives a state had was "determined by adding to the whole Number of free Persons, . . . and excluding Indians not taxed, three fifths of all other Persons"—another euphemism.

The Constitution accommodated slavery for several reasons. Some Southerners, particularly in South Carolina and Georgia, insisted that they would not join a new government that even remotely threatened slavery's existence. Northerners acceded to those demands in part because they simply cared more about creating a new government than they did about eliminating slavery and in part because many believed—or hoped—that slavery would die a natural death as free labor demonstrated its economic advantages.

Slavery did not die out, of course, and even grew in importance in the South, largely for economic reasons. The conventional story, which is mostly correct, is that slavery was most effective in economic terms when slaves were used on large plantations, that the belief in slavery's obsolescence rested on the view that the South would become a land of small farms rather than large plantations, and that technological developments—particularly the invention of the cotton gin to process raw cotton into a form usable for making cloth—revived the prospects for an economy based on cotton plantations. The cotton economy of the early republic also supported a hierarchical social system, with plantation owners superior to ordinary farmers and farmers superior to slaves. Reconciling such a social system with democratic presuppositions that pervaded the nation, including the slave South, could be most easily accomplished by reinforcing the racist dimensions of Southern slavery: Farmers could think that they were equal to planters, at least politically, while both were superior to the enslaved blacks.

Slavery was, among other things, a system of property in which human beings rather than land or goods were the objects of possession, sale, and the like. Whether slaves were treated in legal rules as more like land (real property) or like other possessions (personal property) mattered in determining the liability of third parties for injuries to the slave, and—even more—in determining who would inherit which slaves.

Other questions were more important when issues arose about criminal liability for what slaves did or, as in *State v. Mann*, what owners did to slaves. The central problem for Southern legal thinkers was that they could not deny that slaves were human beings with minds of their own. Even the apparently simplest cases raised conceptual problems. (Of course, describing what the stated rules of law were says very little about what actually happened in the South. The stated rules said that under some circumstances killing a slave was murder, but far more slaves were killed under circumstances fitting the legal definition of murder than defendants were prosecuted.)

Suppose a slave stole property from a neighboring plantation or assaulted a white person. The legal system might have responded by saying that his or her owner should punish the slave. There were two problems with that solution. First, what of the victim? The law could have required the slave's owner to compensate the victims, and that might have been justified by treating the slave's criminal acts as showing that the slave's owner had failed to exercise sufficient control over the slave. Yet that seemed unduly harsh, both to slaves and to their owners. Making the masters pay would have intensified the masters' surveillance of the slaves, making the system even more inhumane than it was. And, no matter how closely they were supervised, slaves were inevitably going to assert their own human will, sometimes by committing what the white community regarded as crimes. Making the masters pay would impose the cost of the slaves' human behavior on the masters when that cost actually flowed from the very existence of slavery.

A second difficulty in connection with crimes committed by slaves is that leaving punishment to the master eliminated any community interest in criminal justice. The whole point of saying that some act was a crime was to express the community's disapproval of the act, but if the community could not do anything about the act, why call it a crime? There was also the problem of the "bad" master, the one who did not care what his slaves did to other people and who would therefore not punish his slaves for the harm they inflicted off the master's plantation.

Everywhere in the slave South, the law imposed criminal liability on slaves for their actions, justifying this by noting that slaves were human beings with all the moral responsibility any human being would have. Treating slaves as human beings for purposes of holding slaves liable for the crimes they committed was easy enough, but what about crimes committed *against* slaves? Could a white person be convicted of killing or assaulting a slave? Aside from the special problem addressed in *State v. Mann* of slaveowners' assaults on their own slaves, most Southern courts drew the natural conclusion that a "stranger," that is, someone other than the slave's owner, could indeed be convicted for killing or assaulting a slave. After all, the courts reasoned, murder was defined as killing a reasonable being, and the fact that slaves were liable for their own crimes showed that they were "reasonable beings" within the ordinary definition of murder. In slavery's early years in the colonies, the statutes treated murders of slaves more leniently than other murders, but by the 1820s, according to historian Thomas Morris, "the trend was clear" in the direction of placing killings of slaves "on a level with the homicide of whites" unless the slave was killed while resisting "mild correction."

North Carolina law in the early 1820s was representative. A 1791 statute said that willful killing of a slave was murder unless the slave was killed while resisting or during moderate correction for misconduct. Later cases held that the statute did not completely displace common law offenses—seemingly a desirable result because the 1791 statute covered only "willful" murders, not manslaughter, which is a killing that occurs when someone is provoked and responds with excessive force. *State v. Tackett* (1820) involved a white defendant charged with killing a slave who lived in Raleigh with his free wife. Tackett and the murdered slave, Daniel, argued about Daniel's wife, and Daniel had threatened Tackett in the past. The trial judge refused to admit evidence that Daniel was generally "insolent and impudent to white people," saying that only evidence about Daniel's insolence to Tackett himself was admissible. Tackett was convicted and sentenced to death. The North Carolina Supreme Court reversed the conviction. Tackett would be guilty of murder if he had not been provoked, but guilty only of manslaughter if he had been. The trial judge had applied the rule derived from cases involving free people, the court said: Only immediate provocation directed at the defendant would lessen the crime from murder to manslaughter. But Tackett's case was different precisely because Daniel was a slave: "[T]he homicide of a slave may be extenuated by acts which would not produce a legal provocation if done by a white person." The jury should have been given a chance to consider whether Daniel's *general* insolence could count as provoking Tackett's violence.

Treating slaves as reasonable beings raised difficult questions, because, as *Tackett* shows, the law usually provided for a number of defenses based on the law's conclusions about how reasonable people would behave under various circumstances. Imagine the following facts. A white person is riding on a country road when he is met by a stranger who demands that the first person move aside. When the first person fails to respond, the stranger assaults him. In response, the first person strikes back, perhaps to the point of severely injuring or even killing the stranger. He is prosecuted for assault or murder. Can he claim that he acted in self-defense or that the charge should be reduced to voluntary manslaughter? Probably yes, because the stranger's demand was unreasonable, the attack by the stranger was unjustified, and the defendant's response was a reasonable one (depending on the amount of force the defendant used to ward off the attack). What of a slave? Facing a beating for what someone thought was misconduct, a slave might resist by striking back. Should the slave's reaction be treated as self-defense against an assault, or should it be treated as an assault with no justification?

North Carolina cases from the 1840s illustrate the problem, indicate some of the solutions, and provide in addition an introduction to Judge Thomas Ruffin's jurisprudence. *State v. Jarrott* (1840) involved a gambling fight. Chatham joined a late-night card game with a number of slaves and free blacks. Chatham began to quarrel with one of the players, and they asked Jarrott to hold the stakes. When the game broke up, Jarrott discovered that one of his coins was missing, and he accused Chatham of stealing it. Chatham offered to let Jarrott search him. Even after the coin was found lying on the ground, Jarrott continued to curse Chatham. Eventually the two men fought, and Jarrott's blow to Chatham's head killed Chatham.

The North Carolina Supreme Court reversed Jarrott's conviction for murder, finding that the offense might have been only manslaughter because Jarrott was provoked. The Court conceded that what counted as provocation had to be different depending on whether the defendant was a slave or a white person because the common law had to be adapted to the "actual conditions of human beings in our society," and "what might be felt by one [that is, the white] as the grossest degradation is considered by the other as but a slight injury." It followed that "[t]he superior rank of the assailant—the habits of humility and obedience which belong to the condition of the slave . . .—clearly forbid that an ordinary assault or battery should be deemed, as it is between white men, a legal provocation." Slaves could not resist, but "it is impossible, if it were desirable, to extinguish . . . the instinct of self-preservation." The slave's "passions ought to be tamed down so as to suit his condition," but "the law would be *savage*, if it made no allowance for passion." A slave assaulted by a stranger would "feel a keen sense of wrong." So if Chatham's attack on Jarrott "endanger[ed] his life or [threatened] great bodily harm" Jarrott's defensive response would reduce the crime from murder to manslaughter. The question was whether Chatham's action "would provoke well-disposed slaves into a violent passion," and that question was for the jury to decide.

The issue of provocation returned to the North Carolina Supreme Court almost a decade later in a case where a slave was provoked by an attack on a friend. Two whites spent an evening getting drunk. They came across two slaves, Caesar and Dick, and said they were patrollers looking for slaves wandering about. They hit the two slaves and, when Dick refused to fetch a whip, they hit Dick harder. Caesar grabbed a fence rail and used it to hit the white men, who left to sleep off the evening's activities. One of them, however, died as a result of Caesar's blows.

A majority of the North Carolina Supreme Court reversed Caesar's murder conviction. Judge Leonard Pearson noted that the passion excited by a white man's observing a friend being assaulted was sufficient provocation to reduce murder to manslaughter, but said that that rule could not be applied directly to slaves, who were "accustomed . . . to constant humiliation." Slaves, already degraded, would not ordinarily find the additional degradation of seeing their friends attacked enough to excite them. If, however, there were "unusual circumstances of oppression," the slave's response might be justified. "The law requires a slave to tame down his feelings to suit his lowly condition, but it would be savage, to allow him, under no circumstances, to yield to a generous impulse" of friendship. Juries would have to decide whether those unusual circumstances existed.

Judge Frederick Nash agreed that the conviction had to be reversed. He emphasized that to deny Caesar the benefit of the rule treating an attack on a friend as sufficient provocation would be a policy decision, properly made by the legislature and not the court. "I am told, that policy and necessity require that a different rule should exist in the case of a slave. Necessity is the tyrant's plea, and policy . . . does not belong to the bench, but to the halls of justice."

As we will see, Judge Ruffin had a quite different view of the proper role of courts. For Ruffin, courts developing the common law always had to take policy considerations into account. True, they had to use "delicacy" in "adjusting the rules of law to new subjects" and should be "cautious against rash expositions, not suited to the actual state of things" (echoing words that, as we will see in the next chapter, he used in *State v. Mann*). Ruffin argued that *Jarrott* and related cases established that an ordinary battery could never constitute provocation for a slave. According to Ruffin, "Negroes—at least the great mass of them—. . . take the most contumelious language without answering again, and generally submit tamely to his buffets, although unlawful and unmerciful." He thought that "slaves are not ordinarily moved to kill a white man for a common beating," because "the great mass of slaves . . . are the least turbulent of all men." Ruffin said that he could identify only a handful of instances where slaves killed whites in fights, which led him to conclude that when a slave did kill a white person, it happened because the slave had "a bad heart—one, intent upon the assertion of equality, social and personal, with the white." That was enough to deny Caesar the provocation defense, but Ruffin went on to note that it was "dangerous to the last degree" to make the defense available: "First denying their general subordination to whites, it may be apprehended that they will end in denouncing the injustice of slavery itself, and, upon that pretext, band together to throw off their common bondage entirely."

We will learn more about Ruffin's views in the next chapters, and I must emphasize that *State v. Mann*, a far more famous case than *State v. Caesar*, was decided two decades earlier. My aim here has been to identify some of the ways in which courts had to confront fundamental issues about the nature of slavery as they decided particular cases. Slave law consisted of the combination of statutes and common law rulings by courts. Statutes left open many questions, which the courts answered by interpreting the statutes or, sometimes, by reverting to the common law. That common law, of course, consisted of judicial decisions. In developing the common law and interpreting the statutes, Southern judges defined the precise content of the law of slavery. Their decisions, as we have seen, rested in the end on a vision of what the judges thought a well-ordered slave society required. Judge Ruffin's opinion in *State v. Mann* fell comfortably within this tradition, but Ruffin's candor, and his talent as a judge, gave his opinion in that case special force.

Understanding the Law of Slavery

The contrast between Lord Mansfield and Judge Ruffin—the one doing something, however limited, to restrain slavery, the other embracing slavery—raises questions not merely about the law of slavery as it developed in the American South but about the role of lawyers in sustaining evil institutions (and of historians in studying those institutions). Since the 1950s and the rise of the civil rights movement, historians have typically found it difficult to avoid a moralistic stance in their discussions of slavery. Treating *State v. Mann* in merely moralistic terms imposes too many limits on what we can learn from the opinion, yet treating it dispassionately may suggest an indifference to the nature of slavery in the American South.

Treating the opinion dispassionately seems necessary if we are to see Judge Ruffin's work as that of an accomplished lawyer. Unlike Lord Mansfield, Judge Ruffin certainly did not think that slavery was an "odious" institution. Ruffin's effort to fit slavery into a system of law does raise questions about the nature of law itself. Modern scholars, reflecting on the experience of law and lawyers during the Nazi era in Germany, have debated whether the system administered by lawyers and judges in a morally monstrous regime truly deserves to be called a "legal" system. For them, the very idea of law conveys some notion of a practice consistent with some broad moral principles. On this view, there could be no such thing as a "law" of slavery, because slavery is inconsistent with the minimum moral requirements for law. Other scholars, often described as positivists, think that there was a law of slavery, just as there was law during the Nazi era. For them, law is sufficiently capacious to accommodate evil practices. Indeed, they suggest, de-moralizing the category *law* has the advantage of depriving a system's supporters of the argument that the system's law deserves some degree of respect simply because it *is* law. Positivists sharply separate law from morality and believe that nothing morally significant follows from describing something as law.

No case study can resolve these deep philosophical questions. Still, examining *State v. Mann* in detail may give us some hints about the answers. But, precisely to avoid prejudging the dispute over the nature of law, the examination probably must be reasonably dispassionate—accepting the moral questions raised by a work taking such a stance.

CHAPTER 2

The Opinion

No one knows when a case begins that it is going to turn out to be a great case. *State v. Mann* started as an ordinary criminal prosecution. A grand jury indicted John Mann for assaulting a slave he had hired. When the case went to trial, the jury was instructed that it could convict Mann if it found that Mann had treated the slave cruelly. The jury convicted Mann, and he appealed to the state supreme court. (At the time, there were only two levels of court in North Carolina: trial courts and the supreme court.) His lawyer urged the court to reverse the conviction because the trial judge's instructions to the jury were an inaccurate statement of the law. By questioning the instructions, the lawyer triggered the supreme court's power to develop the law by examining what instructions should be given. The supreme court agreed that the instructions had been wrong and reversed Mann's conviction with an opinion that made this ordinary criminal case into a great case about the law of slavery.

The Opinion Described

The facts of *State v. Mann*, as described in the official reports, are simple. Elizabeth Jones owned a slave, Lydia, who was hired out for the year 1828 to John Mann in Chowan County, North Carolina. Lydia "committed some small offense," and Mann began to punish her. Lydia started to run off during the punishment. Mann told her to stop, and when she did not, Mann "shot at and wounded her." In the spring of 1829 Mann was indicted for assault and battery. When the case was tried in the fall, the trial judge instructed the jury that if its members were persuaded that the punishment Mann inflicted "was cruel and unwarrantable, and disproportionate to" Lydia's offense, Mann should be found guilty. The jury convicted Mann. The surviving records of the case show that Mann was fined five dollars.

Judge Ruffin's legal analysis began by setting to one side a precedent upholding a prosecution for battery committed on a slave. That case, he wrote, involved "a stranger," that is, someone with no ownership or contract interests in the slave. For Ruffin, *Mann* presented "a different case," because Mann had hired Lydia from Elizabeth Jones. Of course, Ruffin continued, the contract between Mann and Jones might be interpreted to make Mann liable to Jones for "an injury permanently impairing the value of the slave." But Mann's liability to Jones was as irrelevant as was the criminal liability of a stranger. The case involved an *indictment* of someone who had hired a slave for a fixed term, and presented questions about the *state*'s power to regulate the relation of the hirer to the slave.

The trial judge relied on the limited rights Mann had over Lydia, which he called "a special property" in her. The implicit idea is that someone who rents property from another person does not automatically have all the rights over the property that the owner has. Obviously, the contract between the owner and the renter can limit what the renter can do: If Mann had rented a horse from Jones and stated in the contract that he would use the horse only to pull his carriage, he could not—in the absence of extremely special circumstances—use the horse to haul a heavy load from a rock pile. The general law of property might also limit what Mann could do with rented property: He could not borrow money against the value of a rented horse. Contract law and property law limited what Mann could do *with* Lydia. The question in *State v. Mann* was whether the *criminal* law placed any limit on what he could do *to* her.

Judge Ruffin thought not. His legal analysis of that question began where it ended: "Our laws uniformly treat the master or other person having the possession and command of the slave as entitled to the same extent of authority." The law of contract used the idea of special property to deal with how the owner and the hirer dealt with each other; the law of property used that idea to deal with how the hirer dealt with others. The idea of special property was irrelevant when the issue was the relation between the owner or the hirer and the slave (or, as we will see, when the issue was the relation between the state and the owner).

For both owners and hirers, "[t]he object is the same—the services of the slave; and the same powers must be confided." As Judge Ruffin put it, "In a criminal proceeding, and indeed in reference to all other persons but the general owner, the hirer and possessor of a slave, in relation to both rights and duties, is, for the time being, the owner." Ruffin then made the extremely technical observation that the indictment charging Mann with battery might have been defective. If Mann was Lydia's temporary owner for 1828, the indictment, Ruffin suggested, should have charged him with battery on *his own* slave, not on Elizabeth Jones's. Ruffin's first draft of the opinion in *State v. Mann* did not make this point, and, perhaps recognizing how hypertechnical it was, Ruffin moved on to address "the general question" of the *owner's* potential criminal liability for battery on his own slave.

"[T]he Court," wrote Ruffin, "entertains but little doubt" on that question. He observed that no one had previously even argued that a slave's owner could be criminally liable for using excessive force on his own slave and that there had "been no prosecutions of this sort." These facts showed what the "established habits and uniform practice of the country" were, and those habits were "the best evidence of the portion of power deemed by the whole community requisite to the preservation of the master's dominion."

Having introduced the idea of preserving the master's power, Ruffin turned to situations that some might have thought analogous. Slavery was commonly described as a domestic relation. That term actually had two separate meanings. First, slavery was a domestic institution in the sense that it was based on *state* law, not national law. Seeing slavery as domestic in that sense insulated slavery in the states from regulation by the national government. Second, slavery was a domestic institution in the sense that it took place in households. That sense of slavery as a domestic institution provided the analogies Ruffin mentioned: parents and children, tutors and students, masters and apprentices. Ruffin knew that in each of these situations "well-established principles" limited the parents', tutors', and masters' power over their charges. But, Ruffin wrote, "[t]he Court does not recognize their application. There is no likeness between the cases" of parents and children on the one hand and slaveowners and slaves on the other. Ruffin saw "an impassable gulf" between the cases. "The difference is that which exists between freedom and slavery—and a greater cannot be imagined."

For Ruffin, the other domestic relationships had "the end in view [of] the happiness of the youth, born to equal rights with that governor, on whom the duty devolves of training the young to usefulness in a station which he is afterwards to assume among freemen." Ruffin continued, "To such an end, and with such a subject, moral and intellectual instruction seem the natural means; and for the most part they are found to suffice. Moderate force is superadded only to make the others effectual." If "moderate" force failed, it was "better to leave the party to his own headstrong passions and the ultimate correction of the law than to allow it to be immoderately inflicted by a private person." Parents could use moderate force, but they could not use immoderate force. Why? It was better for the child to grow up "headstrong" and be checked himself by the law when he misbehaved. Ruffin did not develop the argument here in detail, but its general form is reasonably clear. The risks *to society* from "headstrong" children were not great enough to outweigh the risks from allowing parents to inflict excessive punishment. Those risks were twofold: first, of course, that children who were only mildly disobedient would be beaten severely, itself a serious harm and perhaps a precursor to their own bad behavior when they grew up; and second, that a parent who developed a character that inflicted severe punishment for minor offenses would not be a good citizen.

Ruffin knew that "[w]ith slavery it is far otherwise." The goal of slavery was not creating good citizens; it was "the profit of the master, his security, and the public safety." Nor was the subject of slavery someone who should grow up to be a good citizen; it was "one doomed in his own person and his posterity, to live without knowledge and without the capacity to make anything his own, and to toil that another may reap the fruits." How could slaves be induced to submit to the conditions under which they lived? Certainly not by the "moral and intellectual instruction" that worked for children: "What moral considerations shall be addressed to such a being to convince him what it is impossible but that the most stupid must feel and know can never be true—that he is thus to labor upon a principle of natural duty, or for the sake of his own personal happiness."

Rather, "such services can only be expected from one who has no will of his own; who surrenders his will in implicit obedience to that of another." Then Ruffin drew the conclusion he thought inevitable: "Such obedience is the consequence only of uncontrolled authority over the body. There is nothing else which can operate to produce the effect. The power of the master must be absolute to render the submission of the slave perfect." For Ruffin, "This discipline belongs to the state of slavery. They cannot be disunited without abrogating at once the rights of the master and absolving the slave from his subjection."

Judge Ruffin was a sophisticated man, and he knew that some slaveowners would behave barbarously. He acknowledged that "in conscience, the law might properly interfere" in such cases. The problem, though, was "to determine where a Court may properly begin." One could provide an answer "in the abstract" to the question of identifying the circumstances under which everyone would agree that a slaveowner behaved cruelly. Ruffin thought that any general answer, any statement of general conditions under which slaveowners might be criminally liable for cruelty to their slaves, "will probably sweep away" all of the masters' powers, because, it seems, *every* power could and would be abused according to any general criteria of abuse. The courts therefore could not even try to develop general criteria for limiting the slaveowners' power over their slaves.

[W]e are forbidden to enter upon a train of general reasoning on the subject. We cannot allow the right of the master to be brought into discussion in the courts of justice. The slave, to remain a slave, must be made sensible that there is no appeal from his master; that his power is in no instance usurped; but is conferred by the laws of man at least, if not by the law of God.

One might say that Ruffin treated the master-slave relation as a *private* one, at least from the law's point of view. To that extent, Ruffin's opinion resonated with skepticism, prevalent in much antebellum law, about what was seen as government—and particularly judicial—intervention in private economic matters. That skepticism was not enough to make the legal system hostile as a general matter to regulating private property, including the master-slave relationship. For Ruffin, there was something special about *judicial* regulation of that relationship. As we will see, he believed that the relationship was *public* as well, subject to community scrutiny through means other than law.

To allow criminal prosecutions of slaveowners for excessive cruelty would imply to the slaves that sometimes their owners were exercising an arbitrary, "usurped" power. A court asked to decide whether a slaveowner had used punishment disproportionate to a slave's offense, as Mann's jury had been asked, would be attempting "to graduate the punishment appropriate to every temper and every dereliction of menial duty," and that would create a "great" danger: "No man can anticipate the many and aggravated provocations of the master which the slave would be constantly stimulated by his own passions or the instigation of others to give; or the consequent wrath of the master, prompting him to bloody vengeance upon the turbulent traitor—a vengeance generally practiced with impunity by reason of its privacy." In light of this danger, Judge Ruffin "disclaim[ed] the power of changing the relation in which these parts of our people stand to each other."

Judge Ruffin then tried to reduce the harshness of his opinion, beginning with the observation that "there is daily less and less occasion for the interposition of the Courts." He listed several reasons: "The protection already afforded by several statutes, that all-powerful motive, the private interest of the owner, the benevolences towards each other, seated in the hearts of those who have been born and bred together, the frowns and deep execrations of the community upon the barbarian who is guilty of excessive and brutal cruelty upon his unprotected slave." These combined to "[produce] a mildness of treatment and attention to the comforts of the unfortunate class of slaves, greatly mitigating the rigors of servitude and ameliorating the condition of the slaves." These factors would continue to affect the slaves' condition "until the disparity in numbers between the whites and blacks shall have rendered the latter in no degree dangerous to the former." The result would be a further relaxation of "the police now existing," by which Ruffin meant the physical force used to subdue slaves.

Relaxing "the police now existing" was a desirable result. The question was how to achieve it. For Ruffin, it would more likely be achieved by waiting for demographic changes and moral reform of the slaveowners than by "any rash expositions of abstract truths by a judiciary tainted with a false and fanatical philanthropy, seeking to redress an acknowledged evil by means still more wicked and appalling than even that evil."

Drafting the Opinion

Ruffin worked hard to set the tone he wanted in his opinion. Two preliminary drafts of the opinion survive. Although the central legal analysis remained basically the same from the first to the last, Judge Ruffin substantially changed the frame within which he placed that analysis. From the beginning he wanted to say how distasteful the case was and that it produced a conflict between "the Judge" and "the man." At first he wrote, "This is one of those cases which a Court will always regret being brought into judgment—One in which principles of policy urge the Judge to a decision in discord with the feelings of the man." His second version began, "It is to be lamented when such cases as the present are brought into judgment." He then glanced northward, it seems, writing, "It is impossible that the reasons on which they go can be appreciated, but when institutions similar to our own exist and are thoroughly understood." (Here Ruffin may have been mindful of antislavery newspapers such as Benjamin Lundy's *Genius of Universal Emancipation*, which had begun circulating in 1821, although antislavery agitation in the North remained at a relatively low level until the 1830s, after *State v. Mann* was decided.) The contrast between "the Judge" and "the man" was sharpened and made more mellifluous as well: "the struggle in the Judge's own breast between the feelings of the man and the convictions of the Magistrate is a severe one."

A shift from a relatively passive phrasing to a relatively active one pervaded Ruffin's editorial revisions of the framing paragraphs. In his first draft, Ruffin followed his contrast between "the Judge" and "the man" with a sentence directing attention away from the courts: "But until the condition of our population be much changed or it shall seem fit to the Legislature to alter the rule, Courts are obliged, however reluctantly, to recognize the rights of the owner to full dominion over the *Slave*." The sentence continued by saying that this full dominion was "essential to their value as property, to the public peace as dependent upon their subordination and, indeed, while slavery in its present form shall continue to exist, as most effectually securing the general protection and comfort of the slave himself."

In the second version, before the reference to the legislature Ruffin placed a new sentence in which he asserted that it was "criminal in a Court to avoid any duty which the laws impose." Still, it was the laws that imposed the duty, not the judge himself. The second draft eliminated the references to the value of slaves as property and, importantly, to the way absolute dominion in owners protected slaves, leaving only the assertion that absolute dominion was "necessary to enforce the obedience and exact the services of the Slave accorded by our law to the owner."

Ruffin's final version was even more forceful. That version put the first sentence in the active voice: "A Judge cannot but lament when such cases as the present are brought into judgment." While still asserting that the laws imposed a duty on the judge, the opinion dropped the mention of the legislature's power to change the law and eliminated the preliminary indication that the rule to be announced was "necessary."

The opinion got stylistically tighter in each revision. In the first draft, Ruffin's presentation of the differences between the subjects of the law of parent and child and the subjects of the law of slavery was followed by a rambling set of sentences that Ruffin pared down in the second draft:

> And who is the subject of this authority? One who has only intelligence and moral feeling enough to make his service reluctant to enable him to understand that the laws, which condemn him to toil for another is unjust, to condemn that injustice and abhor the master who avails himself of it. Can he who has these consciousnesses be prevailed on by moral considerations to perform the functions of servitude? What moral consideration can be presented to him? Is it that there is to be no end to the degradation of himself and his descendants—that, thro' time, his offspring as well as himself are to have no will of their own and that their exertions are never to yield fruit but for a master? Surely every passion, good or bad, of the human heart combine to rebuke the folly of him, who advises or expects the Slave to serve his master upon a principle of natural duty.

The thoughts expressed in this passage survived into the published opinion, but in a far more condensed and rhetorically effective form.

Ruffin ended his first draft with only a gesture in the direction of a conclusion. Its final paragraph, which has the feel of an unfinished performance, noted, "[I]t is with pride as Citizens and sincere joy as men, that we observe every day improvements in the condition of slaves." It referred to statutes requiring owners to give slaves "a comfortable subsistence" and the judicial protection given slaves against assaults by strangers. It observed that public opinion "demands a mitigation of the rigors of slavery, which has not been without the happiest effects upon the feelings of Masters, who now, generally, practice towards the blacks more mildness than formerly and as much indulgence as is consistent with the true interests of both classes and the common safety." The second draft replaced these references with the paragraph, which survived into the final version, describing more effectively the reasons why the conditions of slaves were improving.

Ruffin also developed a more forceful closing paragraph. "I repeat therefore," he wrote, "that we would gladly have avoided this ungrateful question. But Courts are often compelled to act on principles, which outrage individual feeling. This is one instance of it." He continued, somewhat repetitively, "We are obliged therefore to declare, that, until the Legislature shall otherwise order the Courts must recognize the rights of the owner to full dominion over the person of the Slave, unless restrained in particular instances by Statute." His final sentence was to be: "And this we do upon the ground, that such dominion is essential to their value as property and to the public peace, greatly dependent upon their subordination; and while slavery shall continue to exist in its present form as most effectually securing the general protection and comfort of the Slave." The final version improved the rhythm of this sentence, saying that the Court made its decision on the ground that absolute dominion "is essential to the value of the slaves as property, to the security of the master, and the public tranquility, greatly dependent upon their subordination; and, in fine, as most effectually securing the general protection and comfort of the slaves themselves."

Overall, the effect of Ruffin's revisions was to place his own authority behind the harsh rule he was about to announce. The second version, for example, introduced a sentence in which Ruffin asserted, in the first person, "I freely and fully confess my sense of the harshness" of the proposition that "[t]he power of the master must be absolute to render the submission of the slave perfect." The published opinion was crisper and at the same time assumed personal responsibility more directly: "I most freely confess my sense of the harshness of this proposition; I feel it as deeply as any man can; and as a principle of moral right every person in his retirement must repudiate it." The final paragraph of the published opinion similarly asserted personal responsibility, saying not that "we" would gladly have avoided the question but that "I" would gladly have done so. Rather than the abstract and general phrase that "Courts are often compelled to act," Judge Ruffin's final version, while still in the passive voice, did say that the case "being brought to it[,] the Court is compelled to declare" the rule it announced.

The Logic of Slavery in *State v. Mann:*
The Role of Law and the Community

Judge Ruffin's spare style and his acceptance of personal responsibility for the legal rule undoubtedly lent authority to the opinion and were clearly among the reasons abolitionist writers took the opinion in *State v. Mann* as a text central to their critique of the law of slavery. What exactly was Ruffin's legal analysis—his exposition of the logic of slavery? In taking the opinion apart to expose its presuppositions, I will repeatedly quote passages and phrases that I have already presented, because particular phrases take on different meanings when viewed from the various perspectives I develop.

Judge Ruffin's analysis deployed a number of distinctions in an extremely sophisticated way, revealing a great deal about the logic and the law of slavery. One distinction was between statutory law and common law, another was between law and morality, and a third was between law and sentiment. These distinctions interacted in a quite complex manner, so that some aspects of the case, puzzling when we have only one distinction in mind, become less puzzling as we incorporate the others.

Legislative Amelioration of Slavery

We can begin with one of the easier puzzles. As historian Eugene Genovese put it in his classic work *Roll, Jordan, Roll: The World the Slaves Made* (1974), Judge Ruffin's references to "express enactments" that might limit a master's "full dominion" over his slaves seem to express a hope "that the legislature would find a way to remove the high court's dilemma." But if Ruffin's argument was that full dominion was "essential" to preserving slavery, why would he hope for the adoption of statutes limiting that dominion and thereby, it would seem, endangering the master's "security, and the public safety"? The answer must lie in a distinction between limitations on full dominion imposed by judges developing the common law, which would threaten the state's security, and limitations imposed by legislatures, which would not. Ruffin could not have had in mind the thought that slavery was a purely private relation between the master and the slave, not subject to public control through law. Legislative regulation intruded on that relation, yet Ruffin was completely open to the possibility of statutes imposing obligations on masters. Rather, Ruffin must have been concerned about something that distinguished courts, which could not regulate the relation of master and slave, from legislatures, which could.

Ruffin's references to "a train of general reasoning" and to the "[exposition] of abstract truths" are the key. Early-nineteenth-century lawyers took the common law to be an expression of human reason. The common law's principles described the natural order of things in fairly general terms. Skilled lawyers applied reason to the common law's general principles to determine what the legal rule should be in particular circumstances. So, for example, at common law murder was the wrongful killing of a human being, and manslaughter was a wrongful killing committed under circumstances of understandable provocation. What, though, did *wrongful* mean? Suppose a slaveowner attempted to punish a slave for failing to work hard enough, and the slave resisted punishment to the point where the enraged master killed the slave. Was such a killing wrongful? Did the slave's resistance amount to provocation that converted murder into manslaughter? Southern courts provided answers to these questions by considering how the general principles of the common law should be applied in the particular circumstances of slavery in the American South. "General reasoning" directed common law courts to examine what, in the judges' eyes, the social institution of slavery required or permitted. In short, common law reasoning authorized wide-ranging inquiries by judges into the nature of slavery.

Common law judges typically contrasted common law reasoning with the specific requirements of statutes. Statutes, they believed, should be construed narrowly if they sought to modify the common law, because legislatures were not necessarily responding to reason when they acted and because discrete legislative interventions could disrupt the carefully reasoned fabric of the common law. For common law judges, statutes were like islands in the sea of reason; judges would of course apply them, but the statutes had no significant impact on the general contours of the seascape. Specifically, for common law judges statutes could be applied whether or not the judges found them supported by "general reasoning."

Southern legislatures enacted two types of protective statutes, whose characteristics suggest that the broad picture of the distinction between common law as reason and statutory law as intrusion needs some modification. Some statutes were relatively specific, as the preceding discussion indicates, but others were relatively general. The specific ones identified particular forms of cruel behavior. In Georgia just before the Civil War, for example, masters could be criminally prosecuted for inflicting cruel punishments by "beating, cutting, or wounding, or by cruelly and unnecessarily biting or tearing with dogs." North Carolina itself, which never adopted a system of statutory protections for slaves, nonetheless did have a peculiarly backhanded statute: Ordinarily, a slave's owner would be compensated for the slave's death when the slave was executed for criminal conduct, but North Carolina denied compensation to masters who had not given the slave adequate food, clothing, or shelter. The other protective statutes were general ones. For example, in 1852 Alabama's statutes said that a master had to "treat his slave with humanity" and not "inflict upon him any cruel punishment."

Ruffin's reference to "general reasoning" suggests that he assumed that "express enactments" would be of the first, specific type identified above. A statute requiring a master to provide sufficient food or clothing to his slaves would reflect some general propositions about what humanity required, but it would enact a simple rule rather than a general proposition. Courts, in contrast, had to use "general reasoning" to develop the law. And, as Ruffin saw it, the principles that underlay such general reasoning could not justify only some limited set of rules. The principles had to be followed wherever they led—from food, to clothing, to shelter, to protections against physical cruelty, to, perhaps, the conclusion drawn by adherents of "a false and fanatical philanthropy" that slavery itself was unlawful.

Cases such as *Mann* exposed the danger from abstract reasoning. The jurors had been told that they should convict Mann if they were convinced that his action in shooting Lydia while she was trying to escape punishment was "disproportionate" to the offense for which she was being punished. This instruction, according to Ruffin, made it inevitable that courts would "be called on to graduate the punishment appropriate to every temper and every dereliction of menial duty." A slave would be able to complain that *any* physical discipline—a few strokes of the lash—was disproportionate to the particular offense he had committed. It was in this sense that "[t]he slave, to remain a slave, must be made sensible that there is no appeal from his master."

This analysis helps dissolve another mild puzzle about the rule in *State v. Mann*. It was uncontroversial among Southern judges that slaveowners could be prosecuted for murdering their slaves. A decade after *Mann*, Judge Ruffin wrote an opinion upholding the conviction of a master for murdering his own slave. Mira, the slave, was in the late stages of pregnancy when John Hoover began to whip her for failing to obey his orders. Witnesses testified that she could not obey the orders because of her pregnancy. Judge Ruffin recited Hoover's acts:

He beat her with clubs, iron chains, and other deadly weapons, time after time; burnt her, inflicted stripes over and often, with scourges, which literally excoriated her whole body; forced her out to work in inclement seasons, without being duly clad; provided for her insufficient food; exacted labor beyond her strength, and wantonly beat her because she could not comply with his requisitions.

After citing *Mann* for the proposition that the law generally left the question of whether punishment was excessive to the owner's "judgment and humanity," Judge Ruffin insisted that "the master's authority is not altogether unlimited." He must not kill. There is, at the least, this restriction upon his power; he must stop short of taking life.

As with statutory limitations on masters' full dominion, here too we might ask, "If full dominion is necessary for slavery's preservation, doesn't *State v. Hoover* undermine slavery by limiting that full dominion?" Ruffin should be read to assert that the horrendous circumstances of *Hoover* did not matter: He also presented *Mann* as a case involving extremely disturbing circumstances (although of course we cannot eliminate the possibility that truly horrible circumstances affected the cast of mind Ruffin brought to the legal problem), and he said in *Hoover* that what mattered was that the slave had died. What was the difference between assault and murder? The answer is the same as the one that explains why statutory limitations on masters' power were acceptable: The statutory limitations were *discrete* restrictions of the master's authority, and the rule against murdering one's own slaves was similarly discrete. Prosecutions for murder could arise only in quite limited circumstances, while prosecutions for assault and battery raised the possibility of inquiring into the entire range of a master's treatment of his slaves. In particular, a prosecution for murder could succeed only if the slaveowner *intended* to kill the slave. As Ruffin put it in *Hoover,* "the law would doubtless tenderly regard every circumstance" if death "unhappily ensue from the master's chastisement of his slave, inflicted apparently *with a good intent,* for reformation for example, and *with no purpose to take life.*" The requirement of intent sharply limited the occasions on which prosecutions would be possible.

Judge Ruffin's argument against allowing prosecutions for assault was incomplete, though. To whom would a slave "appeal"? After all, what was at stake was criminal liability for excessive punishment, which means that at some point a prosecutor would have to get involved in the case. How would a slave have access to a prosecutor? At this point, Ruffin might have reintroduced a distinction between prosecutions of hirers and prosecutions of owners: A slave believing herself to have been punished excessively could "appeal" to her owner, who might then bring the case to the attention of public authorities. And, it might be thought, an appeal to an owner could not undermine slavery; after all, as we will see, Ruffin believed that *moral* appeals to slaveowners were perfectly compatible with, and even affirmatively valuable for, the preservation of slavery. An injured slave could make no more than a moral appeal to her owner anyway, complaining about maltreatment by the hirer. Ruffin thought he had an answer to this argument. The hired slave's ability to appeal to her owner was fully protected by the rules of civil liability. That is, the slave's owner could sue the hirer for misusing the slave. Criminal prosecutions—an appeal to an institution *beyond* the owner—were unnecessary.

Still, there is an argument supporting criminal prosecutions of hirers as a *supplement* to civil liability. Go back to the case of the stranger—the person with no contractual relationship to the slaveowner—who injures a slave. The slave's owner could of course sue the stranger for damages. Why should the state supplement civil liability with criminal liability? Because at least sometimes the stranger would lack sufficient resources to compensate the owner for the injuries. The prospect of civil liability would deter people with adequate financial resources from harming slaves, but criminal liability ensured that *everyone* felt some deterrent threat.

Now consider the case of a hired slave. Slaveowners would set the rental price with an eye to their assessment of how likely it was that the hirer would injure the slave: The riskier the rental (that is, the more likely the hirer would maltreat the slave), the higher the price. But just as some strangers might not have financial resources, so some hirers might not have enough resources to compensate for the injuries they inflicted, and, perhaps more important, some slaveowners might not be in a good position to determine how likely it was that a hirer would harm the slave. The price the slaveowners set would not fully compensate them for the risk of injury to the slave. Again, the threat of criminal prosecution might reduce the risk of mistreatment to the point where the prices charged for the rental actually reflected the real risks to the slave. Ruffin did not allude to this line of argument, preferring to use *State v. Mann* as the occasion for a general exposition on the necessary dominion of slave*owners*. Chapter 4 explores some possible reasons for Ruffin's choice.

Judge Ruffin alluded to another circumstance in which a slave could realistically believe that an "appeal" beyond the master would be effective—the case of the master widely known in the community to be cruel and deliberately barbaric. The Hoover murder prosecution might be an example. When confronted with a master such as Hoover, the slave might be able to mobilize community outrage against the master. (Of course, in cases of murder, the victims could not "appeal" to anyone, but other slaves owned by the murderous owner could.) Ruffin argued that a community that could be persuaded to bring a prosecution against a barbaric master would also bring that master into disrepute through "frowns and deep execrations," thereby again rendering criminal prosecution unnecessary. The idea of *moral* disapproval was central to Judge Ruffin's overall defense of the result in *State v. Mann*.

State v. Hoover remains to be explained. Judge Ruffin argued that the owner's self-interest in preserving his slaves, coupled with sentimental ties to the slaves and community disapproval of excessive punishment, would reduce barbarity more effectively than would the criminal law. If so, why wouldn't those same factors reduce the number of occasions on which masters murdered their slaves? The answer, developed in more detail in Chapter 3, is that sentiment—both that of the master and those of the community—would inevitably fall short in the case of murder. But, then, why not in the case of barbaric assaults as well? Here too Ruffin's invocation of the distinction between legislation and the common law matters. Murder was a sharply defined category of criminal liability, relatively insensitive to varying circumstances. Courts could uphold murder prosecutions without raising the prospect of intrusive inquiries into the details of the way in which a master treated his slaves.

Before turning in the next chapter to broader implications of *State v. Mann*, it is worth noting, if only to put to one side, another explanation for Judge Ruffin's willingness to accept statutes limiting masters' full dominion and to uphold criminal prosecutions for murder. *State v. Mann* relies at least in part on the need to protect "public safety." Cruel masters were a source of instability and were themselves threats to public safety, because their slaves might become rebellious. The community as a whole therefore had an interest in limiting the power of abusive masters. That interest could justify both statutory limitations on masters' full dominion and common law prosecutions for murder. But, it would seem, it might also justify common law prosecutions for assault and battery. Perhaps the implicit reason for limiting the reach of the community interest in controlling abusive masters was, again, institutional: Judges could be confident that murder prosecutions served the community's interest in public safety, but needed the guidance of legislatures to determine which particular forms of abuse short of murder were similarly threatening.

———

Conclusion

The opinion in *State v. Mann* and Judge Ruffin's revisions as he worked out what he wanted to say reveal that Ruffin saw the opinion as dealing specifically with the judicial role in developing the law of slavery, and not with a broader "logic of slavery," as readers from Stowe to Genovese have taken it. Yet those readers were not wrong. In distinguishing between courts and legislatures as institutions for regulating slavery, Judge Ruffin implicitly relied on deep-lying notions about how slavery was embedded in the life of Southern communities. Chapter 3 examines those notions.

Scholars and *State v. Mann*

Scholars have been intrigued by *State v. Mann* because Judge Ruffin's opinion brings into view a large number of issues that have broad significance for understanding not merely Southern law but Southern slavery and even law itself. What makes Judge Ruffin's opinion so rich is that his holding—that Mann's conviction should be reversed because the jury should have been instructed that a hirer cannot be found guilty of an assault on the hired slave—is supported by a variety of underlying reasons, each of which radiates into other areas of interest to historians and lawyers. This chapter explores several of the issues discussed by historians, economists, and legal academics.

The "Moral-Formal Dilemma"

Judge Ruffin's distinction between "the feelings of the man" and "the duty of the magistrate" and his statement that "every person in his retirement must repudiate" the proposition that the "power of the master must be absolute" suggest some questions about how judges respond to what they believe—"in their retirement"— to be unjust legal rules. When Ruffin retired from the Supreme Court in 1852, his letter of resignation said, "I have administered the law as I understood it, and to the ends of suppressing crime and wrong, and upholding virtue, truth, and right."

Ruffin's statements suggest that he was experiencing what law professor Robert Cover calls a "moral-formal dilemma." Cover describes such dilemmas as forcing judges to choose between morality and "formal principles" specifying the role of the judge and "the sense of the judicial craft." (Cover uses a concept of formalism that is similar to one used by legal historian Morton Horwitz, who distinguishes between formalism and instrumentalism in antebellum legal thought and practice. Cover's concern about the "moral-formal dilemma" is different from Horwitz's concerns, which I discuss in Chapter 4.)

Cover's primary focus is on judges who asserted that as "men" they opposed slavery but were bound by their legal duties as "magistrates" to enforce laws that preserved or even extended slavery's reach. Cover argues that judges faced with a moral-formal dilemma engaged in various tactics to reduce the cognitive dissonance they experienced. The most important, probably, was what Cover calls the "[e]levation of the formal stakes (sometimes coupled with minimization of the moral stakes)." In escalating the formal stakes, the judge claimed that disregarding the law or tempering it with justice would undermine the entire value of law in preserving social order. So, for example, Cover quotes Justice Lemuel Shaw of Massachusetts defending the role of precedent in law as "absolutely necessary to the peace, union and harmonious action of the state and general governments."

Cover's interest in antislavery judges means that he pays slight attention to *State v. Mann*. He does describe Ruffin as "the most eloquent spokesman for a stern necessity, requiring an unflinching, conscious disregard of natural justice," which suggests that he sees Ruffin as experiencing some version of the moral-formal dilemma. On the "moral" horn we find Ruffin's assertion that "moral right" requires one to "repudiate" the idea of full dominion and his other comments on the harshness of that idea. On the "formal" horn, Ruffin's opinion repeatedly invokes "the law" as an external constraint on the judges, arising from necessity. The court, Ruffin wrote, could not "avoid any responsibility which the laws impose" and which arose out of "things inherent in our political state" or, as he put it a few paragraphs later, out of "the actual condition of things."

We can also find in *State v. Mann* both the escalation of the formal stakes and the minimization of the moral ones. On the formal side, "the danger would be great, indeed," if the courts were allowed to examine whether punishment was excessive. Full dominion was "essential" to "the public tranquility," which was "greatly dependent upon [the slaves'] subordination." A more complex and subtle version of the formal horn is Ruffin's reference to "a false and fanatical philanthropy, seeking to redress an acknowledged evil by means still more wicked and appalling than even that evil." This reference is ambiguous. Ruffin's readers may have understandably taken "philanthropy" to refer to abolitionism, with Ruffin criticizing the "fanatical philanthropy" of abolitionism for seeking to redress the evil of abuse of slaves by masters by the "more wicked" means of abolition. Yet describing abolition as the "means" is a bit odd. The "philanthropy" of abolitionism is not a "means" to some other end, but is rather the end itself. An alternative reading of Ruffin's reference would be that he is concerned with a "philanthropy" that uses the courts and general reasoning as a means to the end of abolition. That is precisely what Cover means in referring to an escalation of the formal stakes.

On the moral side, Ruffin's exposition on the "mildness of treatment and attention to the comforts of the unfortunate class of slaves" expressly minimized the moral unattractiveness of slavery, concluding that factors other than law were "greatly mitigating the rigors of servitude and ameliorating the condition of the slaves."

Yet there is something odd in treating *State v. Mann* as an example of a judge grappling with the moral-formal dilemma. (Cover himself does not do so.) Most notably, Judge Ruffin rather clearly distanced himself from slavery's opponents. The opinion's second sentence reads, "It is impossible that the reasons on which [cases like *Mann*] go can be appreciated, but where institutions similar to our own exist and are thoroughly understood." This appears to refer to Northerners and to critics of slavery who did not thoroughly understand it. Even more strongly, the "false and fanatical philanthropy" to which Ruffin referred had *something* to do with abolitionism, if only that readers such as Stowe and Goodell were likely to think that it referred to them and their allies. Ruffin, that is, was not writing as

{ *Slave Law in the American South* }

a judge who felt himself on the moral horn of the dilemma by sympathy for abolition and who responded by invoking the formal horn. He was writing as an unabashed defender of slavery. Ruffin did not believe that the law, which was moral, condemned slavery as immoral. Rather, he faced a conflict *within* morality, between slavery understood to be moral and the law understood to be moral as well.

What, then, to make of the tension evident in the opinion? One possibility is that Judge Ruffin was writing in the midst of a transition in the slave South's defense of slavery. As a young man Ruffin had received a letter from his father describing slavery as an evil, but one that his father saw no way of eliminating. Others in the South during the early nineteenth century described slavery as a necessary evil, with slightly different overtones than the view offered by Ruffin's father. By the late 1820s, though, Southerners had become a bit more forthright about slavery. Eventually they came to describe slavery as a positive good. The transition from characterizing slavery as an evil to characterizing it as a good had not been completed when Ruffin wrote *State v. Mann*, but the tensions within the opinion might reflect the uncertain state of the defense of slavery in 1830: *That* slavery had to be defended was clear; *how* it was to be defended was far less so.

Another possibility is that Judge Ruffin was looking deeply into the heart of slavery, describing what he found there, and asking his readers to accept the facts by changing not slavery, but their view of morality. Here one might note the juxtaposition Ruffin created between a person "in his retirement" and "the actual state of things." The man in his retirement might be a bookish scholar in his library, or a planter relaxing at the end of the day in his drawing room, places where the real world does not intrude and in which moral speculation can be untethered from reality. But precisely because such speculation was abstract, people engaged in "the actual state of things" should avoid it. On this reading, Ruffin was asking his readers to engage in a process of moral transformation, ridding themselves of a sentimentality that obstructed their understanding that slavery was actually morally defensible. On this reading, Ruffin's description of the threat posed to social stability by criminal prosecutions of masters for assaulting their slaves was not an escalation of the moral stakes; it was a simple description.

This reading of Ruffin's opinion, though defensible, has some flaws. Goodell noted in 1853 that *State v. Mann* was written in 1830, "before there was any excitement raised on the slave question," but Goodell overstated the absence of "excitement" on the issue of slavery in 1830. Sentiment for slavery's abolition went back to the period before the Revolution. The American Colonization Society was organized in 1817, and an astute observer (or a very nervous Southerner) could discern the glimmerings of a more radical abolitionism by the late 1820s. Still, Goodell was correct in asserting that the slavery issue had not emerged with anything like the force it took on shortly after 1830, when Nat Turner's rebellion (1831) and debates over abolishing slavery in Virginia (1831–32) raised the issue's salience. *State v. Mann* was decided before there was any need to steel slaveowners against a sentimentality pervading the culture that might lead them to find abolitionism attractive. Perhaps more important, Ruffin's statement that the mitigation and amelioration of slavery was "greatly to be desired" shows that Ruffin did not personally endorse actual harshness in the operation of slavery as an institution. A legal rule that shielded masters' brutality from legal scrutiny was essential, and every defender of slavery should understand that, but brutal behavior was not. Ruffin's focus, that is, was on *the law* of slavery, not on slavery as a social practice.

Judge Ruffin's attention to the appropriate roles of courts and legislatures in developing rules responding to humanitarian concerns suggests another perspective on his opinion. Goodell wrote that Ruffin's contrast between "the man" and "the magistrate" meant that "slavery requires of its magistrates to trample upon their own manhood." Ruffin obviously had no such meaning in mind. Instead, he was arguing that "the man" could protect slaves by means that were barred to "the magistrate." We can call this argument one that offers an *institutional* perspective. Judge Ruffin might have been primarily interested in dividing responsibility for slavery, taken as a whole, among different institutions, of which the common law was only one. Slavery's morality was ensured not by law but by other institutions, and the law's morality was preserved by ensuring that the law stood apart from slavery.

An Economic Analysis of the Problem

After mentioning the "protection already afforded by several statutes," Ruffin turned to institutions *other than* law. The first was "that all-powerful motive, the private interest of the owner." Here Ruffin argued, reasonably enough, that slaveowners had an economic interest in ensuring that their slaves were productive. That interest would lead most slaveowners to use only the force sufficient to guarantee that the slave would be productive, and that degree of force would rarely injure the slave permanently.

Self-interest is often the domain of economists, and economic historians have indeed examined Southern slavery. Robert Fogel and Stanley Engerman provoked a large controversy when they published *Time on the Cross: The Economics of American Negro Slavery* in 1974. Fogel and Engerman used economic tools to support the conclusion that slavery was profitable, in the sense that slaveowners made as much, or more, by investing in slaves as they could have made by investing in other forms of farm or industrial production. As economists, Fogel and Engerman treated masters' decisions about what food to give their slaves and how much to punish them as economic decisions that could be explained by examining whether the investment in food and the punishment inflicted made the slaves more productive. The critics of Fogel and Engerman argued against their statistical analysis but seemingly were more concerned that by asserting that slavery was financially profitable Fogel and Engerman were somehow defending it. Fogel and Engerman's analysis could have been taken as a serious *criticism* of profit making, though: If an institution as obviously immoral as slavery was compatible with profit-making, perhaps other profit making activities were also immoral.

We can understand an economic analysis of slavery in many ways. Most economists rely on *institutions* of competition to account for individual behavior. People who do not behave in certain ways will make smaller profits than others and will be unable to sustain their operations—and their finances—in the face of competition. Other economists, and probably most non-economists, think that economics is about *motivations:* People behave as they do because they want to make as much money as they can. This, of course, distorts even a motivational approach to economic rationality. Economists would say that, to the extent they are concerned with motivation, they think that people behave as they do because they want to maximize whatever it is that they value. For many people, that will be money. But economists would have no problems understanding a person who decided that it was worth giving up some money income that could be made by investing in Northern industries to sustain the lifestyle of a country gentleman—or of a Southern slaveowner.

Fogel and Engerman's analysis was controversial in part because they were taken to be giving a motivational account of slaveowners' behavior. That is, their critics thought that Fogel and Engerman were arguing that slaveowners provided adequate amounts of food to their slaves because they understood that doing so would make the slaves more productive. Judge Ruffin's invocation of self-interest as a reason for expecting humane treatment of slaves suggests a similar motivational account.

Other economists, and lawyers influenced by economic theory, have developed a general economic approach to law. The economic analysis of law attempts to explain how legal rules promote economic efficiency, defined for these purposes as achieving, at the lowest possible cost, as many preferences as people have. Economist Jenny Bourne Wahl has used economic analysis to explain the rules of Southern slave law while acknowledging the obvious, that the Southern slave law did not take the preferences of slaves into account in its attempt to maximize the achievement of people's desires. Law-and-economics analysis attempts to make economic sense of legal rules. In a market-oriented society, for example, the legal rules will promote the production of the kinds and amounts of goods that people want. In the slave South, the legal rules promoted the smooth operation of the slave system.

Wahl focuses primarily on the liability of hirers *to masters* for various things that could go wrong. So, for example, courts would enforce contracts of hire strictly if the contract specified that the hired slave was to be used for a particular purpose and the hirer used the slave for something else, even something not intrinsically more dangerous. A contract might say that the slave was to be used in a particular county, and the slave might be injured while working in a neighboring county. Courts would award damages without requiring the slave's owner to show that sending the slave out of county was particularly dangerous because the slave's owner, not knowing about working conditions elsewhere, would have increased the rental price to take account of the unknown risks.

What would self-interest tell us about slave hirers? With respect to hirers such as Mann, self-interest in preserving the value of the slave operated indirectly, through the rental price. The most obvious case is the renter with a reputation for brutal treatment, who would have to pay a higher price to rent a slave than other renters did. Brutal hirers might have to pay a lot to rent a slave, but the high price alone would not eliminate brutality, if a slaveowner was willing to let his slave be brutalized. It might take some time for a hirer to get a reputation for brutality, and meanwhile the *owner's* self-interest would be insufficient to protect the hired slave, because the owner would not charge a high enough price for the rental. Wahl also notes the possibility, discussed earlier, that the criminal law might have been needed to protect masters' interests against damage to their slaves inflicted by people who could not afford to compensate the masters. She quotes an 1823 North Carolina case upholding an indictment: "The value of slave property must be much impaired, for the offenders can seldom make any reparation in damages." With some modification, this analysis might support indictments of slave hirers as well. Consider the owner considering hiring out a slave to a person known to be brutal. The owner might charge a relatively high price, taking into account the hirer's reputation and the risk that the hirer would treat the slave so badly that the slave's value would be cut in half. That amount of harm was not inevitable, though.

The hirer might be able to pay the high rental price and yet be unable to compensate the slave's owner if the harm actually occurred.

The case of the slaveowner himself was different. Wahl's economic analysis leads her to conclude that masters were held liable—essentially, through criminal proceedings—only when their behavior toward their own slaves imposed costs on the rest of the community. "[C]ourts and legislatures proscribed some cruel treatment by masters for fear that unchecked slave abuse could have led to unpleasant scenes of public beatings, pilfering, and insurrection." Slaves given inadequate food would forage in the neighborhood and steal from others. As one court put it, laws requiring provision of food resulted from "public sentiment" and were "necessary to protect property from the depredation of famishing slaves." Slaves routinely beaten to excess might try to escape, or worse. In the words of a Virginia judge, "oppression and tyranny, against which there is no redress, may drive [slaves] to despair" and rebellion.

The difficulty with economic analysis is that it can account for anything. Consider the issue Judge Ruffin thought implicated in *State v. Mann*, the potential criminal liability of a slaveowner for cruel treatment, short of killing, of his own slave. Such treatment could readily cause external costs, that is, increased risks to people other than the slaveowner. As noted, excessive cruelty could transform slave character, making slaves potential rebels whose uprisings would threaten the entire community, and a master might create an unpleasant scene in public while beating his slave. On this analysis, then, Judge Ruffin was wrong, and the common law of criminal liability was not economically efficient. But, an economist might also say, the external costs of a master's cruelty were probably not large, and deploying the community's power through the criminal law is itself costly—both in terms of resources devoted to investigation and prosecution and in terms of mistaken prosecutions, where on examination the master was not "excessively" cruel. So, on *this* interpretation of the underlying economic facts, Judge Ruffin was correct, and the common law of criminal liability *was* economically efficient. An analysis so flexible is essentially unilluminating.

In contrast, abolitionist writer Theodore Dwight Weld's analysis of the role of self-interest in generating protections for slaves is complex and probing. Responding to the claim that "it is for the interest of the masters to treat their slaves well," Weld began, "So it is for the interest of the drunkard to quit his cups. . . . The whole history of man is a record of real interests sacrificed to present gratification. If all men's actions were consistent with their best interests, folly and sin would be words without meaning." Weld then turned to the narrower idea of "pecuniary interest." Here, he said, "though the love of money is strong, yet appetite and lust, pride, anger and revenge, the love of power and honor, are each an overmatch for it." Weld emphasized that long-term pecuniary interests would often succumb to "[t]he strongest feeling of any moment." For Weld, the evidence that Southern slaveowners were "proverbial for lavish expenditures, never haggling about the *price* of a gratification," showed that "love of money" was not the slaveowner's ruling passion. "Love of money gets a snatch at the scepter as well as the rest," but only as a matter of chance.

Weld then enumerated categories of slaves with whom short-term pecuniary interest would not lead to good treatment: the old, the worn out, the incurably diseased, and, notably, hired slaves. Coupled with an analysis of why masters had a pecuniary interest in overworking their slaves, this list led Weld to turn around the proposition offered by slavery's defenders: *"It is for the interest of slaveholders, upon their own principles, and by their own showing,* TO TREAT CRUELLY *the great body of their slaves."* Here Weld's polemical interests got the better of him, because he could not, and did not, contend that *every* slave in all these categories was inhumanely treated (beyond, of course, the inhumanity inherent in slavery itself). But to the extent that masters treated their slaves with some degree of humanity even when short-term pecuniary interests pointed in the other direction, some motivation other than pecuniary interest had to be at work.

With respect to both slaveowners and slave hirers, then, economic interest alone would not be enough. We can now return to Judge Ruffin's opinion. After mentioning self-interest, Ruffin moved on, noting "the benevolences towards each other, seated

in the hearts of those who have been born and bred together."
Economic self-interest operated in the market. The "benevolences" Ruffin referred to, in contrast, arose from the master-
slave relationship itself. The idea is clear enough: A slaveowner
who has seen a slave grow from infancy into productive labor is
likely to regard that slave as a person, entitled as such to decent
treatment within the institution of slavery. Of course, the limitations of the idea are clear as well: The motive of benevolence
would not operate when slaveowners were dealing with recently
acquired slaves, nor would it operate when a slave was rented out
to a hirer who had no preexisting ties to the slave.

The Role of Sentiment and Honor

Yet Ruffin's reference to a motive "seated in the heart" evokes a
familiar image about institutions. Law, as Ruffin put it, involved
"general reasoning," while benevolence arose in the heart. The
distinction here parallels one drawn in some Marxist discussions
of the contrast between capitalism and slavery as economic and
social systems. One need not accept all the premises of Marxism
or the economic analysis and predictions of classical Marxist theory for capitalist society to see how Marx's distinction between
labor and labor power might illuminate the way in which sentiment played a special role in the ideology of slavery.

Marx distinguished between a person's labor power and his
labor. For Marx, labor power was an undifferentiated characteristic of all workers, something that could be reduced to the single measure of the wage. Labor power is the worker's capacity to
work, divorced from everything else one might say about the
worker. Relations in the capitalist market are confined to exchanges of money for labor power, and the purchaser cares nothing about what happens to the worker outside the workplace.
Labor, in contrast, is what a person does in all aspects of his life.
Slavery is an economic and social system in which the slaveowner
purchases the slave, not simply the slave's labor power. This creates a totalistic relationship between the owner and the slave, in

which the slaveowner knows of and is interested in the slave considered as an entire person by reason of economic and social relationships. A capitalist employer can be sentimental about the workers' lives only at the risk of making bad economic decisions about the use of their labor power. In contrast, a slaveowner, on this view, *must* develop ties of sentiment rather than, or in addition to, ties of economic maximization because of the structure of the master-slave relationship. As Eugene Genovese put it in his summary of the ideology of the Southern eccentric George Fitzhugh, relationships in slave society were *organic*. And, finally, in organic relations the heart plays a role alongside the mind.

Judge Ruffin alluded to this sort of thinking in an address he delivered in 1855, after he retired from the Supreme Court. After discussing the economic reasons masters had for treating their slaves well, Ruffin turned to the "stronger tie" between master and slave. "Often born on the same plantation, and bred together, they have a perfect knowledge of each other, and a mutual attachment." Critics of slavery, he said, mistakenly "confound authority in the private relations, though it be that of a slave-owner, with the absolute power of a prince on a throne." The reason for the mistake was that "[a] political despot is separated from his subjects. He knows them not, nor loves them." In contrast, "authority in domestic life, though not necessarily, is naturally considerate, mild, easy to be entreated, and tends to an elevation in sentiment in the superior which generates a humane tenderness for those in his power." Problems arose only when slaves resisted their owners, which they rarely did "if kept to themselves, unprompted from without."

The opposition between the mind and the heart, law and sentiment, was common in the antebellum period, as intellectual historian Perry Miller showed. What, though, were the *institutions* of sentiment? Judge Ruffin mentioned one in *State v. Mann*, in describing "the frowns and deep execrations of the community upon the barbarian who is guilty of excessive and brutal cruelty to his unprotected slave." Ruffin wrote that "bloody vengeance" on slaves who resisted an owner's direction was "generally practiced with impunity by reason of its privacy," but it is important here to note that Ruffin did not believe that the barbarians' conduct was private in some normative sense, deserving to be insulated from any form of consideration by the community. The community could act when acts of brutality came to its attention, whether through reports by slaves to their owners about a hirer's brutality or through the community's rumor mill fed, in part, by a brutal owner's slaves themselves.

One might think that criminal prosecutions were the way in which the community execrated barbarians. Instead, the frowns came from the community organized *outside* the law. Slaveowners felt the force of the community's condemnation because they were people of honor. Bertram Wyatt-Brown treated Southern honor in his book with that title, which has become a classic. For Wyatt-Brown, honor was a system with three components: "the inner conviction of self-worth, . . . the claim of that self-assessment before the public, . . . [and] the assessment of the claim by the public, a judgment based upon the behavior of the claimant." For Wyatt-Brown, "submission to public evaluation prevented outrageous haughtiness and encouraged affability." In an extremely complex way, honor also constrained brutal behavior, at least beyond the bounds of what the community regarded as acceptable.

Wyatt-Brown begins his discussion of the slaveowner's criminal responsibility by noting that "[p]olicing one's own ethical sphere was the natural complement of the patriarchal order" and entailed "unchecked freedom to be one's own final authority." But of course unchecked freedom is freedom that can be abused. The difficulty for the criminal law, as Judge Ruffin's argument regarding the degrees of provocation suggested, was to distinguish between abuse and justifiable responses to threats to a master's honor. Wyatt-Brown writes that "masters often acted out of genuine fear, either for their lives or for plantation command," and "[f]ellow whites . . . would have despised a squeamish slaveholder who was unable to make his will felt." Slaveowners had to "prove manliness" through administering discipline to their slaves. The problem, though, was that, as Wyatt-Brown puts it, sometimes masters "[m]omentarily . . . felt helpless, shamed, and driven to inarticulate fury," producing a reaction that, on calm reflection, the master and the community would both regard as improper. In Genovese's words, "Much cruelty occurred because average masters lost their tempers—something any other master had to excuse unless he saw himself as a saint who could never be riled." Legal rules that allowed the community to prosecute masters for dishonorable actions that might have been taken to defend honor would intrude on the master's "ethical sphere." For Genovese, "moral pressure, if it could not prevent savages from acting savagely, did set a standard of behavior to which men who cared about their reputations tried to adhere."

Like Judge Ruffin, Wyatt-Brown does not take the law as the sole expression of the community's sense of honor. "Although men possessed the right to do as they pleased in regard to race control," Wyatt-Brown writes, "what they pleased to do had to conform to the guidelines that local society provided." Legal historian Sally Hadden has explored in great detail Wyatt-Brown's primary example: masters who tried to make their plantations "the prime center of group loyalty" by keeping out the slave patrols that the community used to ensure that slaves were properly docile. In the end, Hadden shows, masters' resistance was overcome, because the proper regard of the community was essential to the preservation of the very honor that the masters sought to demonstrate.

Wyatt-Brown's subtle analysis points out that honor was two-sided. A man of honor, it might be said, could never accept as controlling the community's judgment that he had behaved dishonorably, but he could also never completely reject that judgment—as long as he hoped to remain part of the community. Submitting to the community's judgment would be demonstrating the "groveling, obsequiousness, and slavishness" that honorable men sought from their inferiors; resisting it would separate the master from the very community in whose judgment honor consisted. The Southern system of honor, then, was filled with "ambiguity and potential explosiveness." It could not solve the problem that one master's brutality posed in a community of honorable men.

The Southern ethos of honor was the source of the "frowns and deep execrations of the community" on which Judge Ruffin relied to keep masters under control. But how could he reconcile that with his argument that "[t]he slave, to remain a slave, must be made sensible that there is no appeal from his master"? Why, that is, might not slaves "appeal" to the community, asking that it invoke its code of honor, if not its legal code, against an abusive master? Wyatt-Brown suggests, indirectly, one answer, when he notes that men charged with crimes against slaves—their own or others'—"usually received acquittals, pardons, or light sentences." One might infer from this that the community's code of honor could be invoked only when disapprobation was essentially universal. In contrast, slaves appealing to "the law" might actually mobilize only a segment of the community against the offending slaveowner. Still, the prosecutor and, particularly, the jury (as we will see in Chapter 4) might be reasonably good proxies for the community as a whole. The conditions for invoking the code of honor as an institution were not sharply distinct from the conditions for invoking the legal code. Judge Ruffin's argument, then, was incomplete.

Abolitionist writers found Judge Ruffin's reliance on the legislature and on honor to guarantee slavery's humane operation hypocritical. Goodell, for example, noted in connection with the possibility of an indictment for a statutory violation, "[W]hy was not the defendant . . . indicted for the *shooting* of Lydia, if there *existed* any statute forbidding such an outrage? And if *not*, where is the protection?"

Weld, writing before Goodell, was if possible even more outraged. Weld devoted several dozen pages to refuting the proposition that "public opinion is a protection to the slave." Weld described "the legal code of the slave states" as an "unerring index of the public opinion of slaveholders towards their slaves." Because law making was "a formal, deliberate act, performed by persons of mature age, embodying the intelligence, wisdom, justice and humanity of the community," enacted laws were for Weld "a true index of the permanent feelings, the settled *frame of mind*, cherished by the community upon those subjects, and towards those persons and classes whose condition the laws are designed to established." Weld compiled statutes showing what masters could do to slaves, and summarized his reaction to these statutes: "Brazen effrontery, hypocrisy, and falsehood! . . . '[P]ublic opinion' does pertinaciously *refuse* to protect the slaves; not only so, it does itself persecute and plunder them all." Weld's equation of public opinion with law misled him, though. Consider his treatment of the Louisiana case of *Jourdan v. Martin.* In Weld's words (and with his emphasis):

A slave of the plaintiff had been deprived of his *only eye,* and thus rendered *useless,* on which account the court adjudged that the defendant should pay the plaintiff his full value. The case went up, by appeal, to the Supreme Court. Judge Mathews, in his decision said, "[W]hen the defendant had paid the sum decreed, the slave ought to be placed in his possession,"— adding, "the judgment making full compensation to the owner *operates a change of property.*" He adds, "The principle of humanity which would lead us to suppose, that the mistress whom he had long served, would treat her miserable blind slave with more kindness than the defendant to whom the judgment ought to transfer him, CANNOT BE TAKEN INTO CONSIDERATION!" The full compensation of the mistress for the loss of the services of the slave, is worthy of all "consideration," even to the utmost farthing; "public opinion" is omnipotent for *her* protection; but when the food, clothing, shelter, fire and lodging, medicine and nursery, comfort and entire condition and treatment of her poor blind slave, throughout his dreary pilgrimage, is the question—ah! that, says the mouthpiece of the law, and the representative of "public opinion," "CANNOT BE TAKEN INTO CONSIDERATION." Protection of slaves by "public opinion" among slaveholders!

The Louisiana Supreme Court's argument, read in the light cast by *State v. Mann,* was that *the law* could not properly take into account the feelings of humanity that would undoubtedly lead the slave's longtime owner to treat him better than the new owner would. The new owner might, from his own feelings of humanity, treat the "poor blind slave" decently, though not as well as the former owner would. As the court put it in sentences not quoted by Weld, "Cruelty and inhumanity ought not to be presumed against any person. A remedy for them can only be applied, if they are legally proven." If the new owner did not treat the slave decently, the community—public opinion expressed outside the law—would condemn the master, and in extreme cases so might the law.

Weld picked up on the idea that many outrages were committed in private and would not become known to the community: "[I]f a man is restrained from certain acts through fear of losing his character, should they become known, he will not voluntarily destroy his character by *making them known*, should he be guilty of them." Weld thought it was "sheer fiction" to think that Southern public opinion "so frowns on cruelty to the slaves, that *fear of disgrace* would restrain from the infliction of it, were there no other consideration." Weld cited innumerable advertisements for runaway slaves in which the slaves were described in terms demonstrating to him that they had been subjected to inhumane treatment, through brandings, beatings, shootings, and more. Slaveowners who were willing to display to the public what they had done to their slaves in the course of attempting to recover the slaves could not, Weld believed, actually fear that their self-betrayal would injure their character in their communities. After reciting advertisements for runaway female slaves, which contained detailed descriptions of their bodies, Weld commented that all this did not "[impair] in the least, the standing in the community of the shameless wretches who thus proclaim their own abomination. That such things should not at all affect the standing of such persons in society, is certainly no marvel."

Weld made a powerful case that fear of the frowns and execrations of the community would be less effective than Judge Ruffin appeared to think. Communities across the South, it seemed, were less outraged by apparently barbarous conduct than Judge Ruffin thought they would be—although the very fact that Mann was convicted shows that some in Mann's own community were indeed outraged. To put it another way, just as self-interest would not fully eliminate the occasions on which slaveowners might mistreat their slaves—with the measure of mistreatment being the standard of the community—neither would sentiment mobilized through the community.

The Role of Religion

Judge Ruffin failed to mention another institution for controlling masters' misconduct, perhaps because the institution was so pervasive that its function literally went without saying. That institution was religion as practiced in churches throughout the South. As Genovese puts it, religion is a "symbolic rendering of man's moral experience" that "proceeds intuitively and imaginatively." Religion's metaphors and preachings describe "the antagonisms between the life of the individual and that of society." As Genovese argues, the Christianity that pervaded the South was simultaneously a conservative force, separating God's domain from Caesar's, and a transformative one, holding out the promise of a better world. That Southern Christianity was also Protestant gave it an individualistic focus, because for Protestants each person was responsible for his own fate. This focus, though, blurred the organic character of slavery as presented by its most astute defenders such as Fitzhugh. In Genovese's words, "the Christian churches have fought to embody an acceptance of the dignity and sanctity of the human personality in submission to a collective discipline that alone can guarantee the freedom of the individual in a world haunted by the evil inherent in the nature of man."

Roll, Jordan, Roll, where Genovese offered these thoughts, was about slaves and, in this context, their religion. But his observations apply to the slaveowners as well. Legal and religious rhetoric alike treated slaves as human beings. For example, no one doubted that slaves had sufficient moral personality to be liable for the crimes they committed. Even more, the *reason* masters could be prosecuted for killing their slaves was, as the Mississippi Supreme Court put it in 1821, that slaves were "reasonable and accountable beings and it would be a stigma upon the character of the state, and a reproach to the administration of justice, if the life of a slave could be taken with impunity. . . . Has the slave no rights, because he has been deprived of his freedom? He is still a human being." Slaves, then, were humans subjected to the collective discipline of slavery.

What was the collective discipline to which masters were subject? The Mississippi Supreme Court's opinion went on to note, as Judge Ruffin later did in *Mann*, that in Mississippi "even cruelty to slaves, much less the taking away of life, meets with universal reprobation." Here again, the collective was the organized community. But, even more, so was organized religion.

By the 1820s the leading religious denominations in the South had reached an accommodation with slavery. In historian Anne Loveland's words, they agreed to treat slavery "as a political, not a moral or religious matter." The churches would not fight slavery as an institution, but they would insist on exemplary behavior by masters. As historian Douglas Ambrose puts it in analyzing sermons by Southern ministers from 1750 to 1800, the Southern clergy worked hard at instilling the sentiments that would "ensure that [slaveowners] conformed to socially acceptable standards." According to Ambrose, "ministers hoped to eliminate the abuses of slavery as a system by convincing masters that their duties as Christians trumped their economic and legal power over their slaves." Another historian summarizes this view: "The major responsibility of a good man who owned slaves would be to see that they also 'knew Christ' and adopted the 'goodness' of their master." The churches, according to Loveland, "were forced to rely principally on exhortation as a means of ameliorating the condition of the slaves."

But what was to be done when masters failed to heed the exhortations? Ambrose's detailed analysis of sermons in which Southern ministers elaborated on what it meant for a master to be a head of a household containing dependents—white women, the master's children, and slaves—provides the beginnings of an answer cast in religious terms. The ministers argued that masters stood in relation to their dependents just as God did to the masters. The masters had a religious duty to ensure their dependents' salvation because the dependents, including the slaves, were morally equal to the masters in God's eyes. As one pamphlet quoted by Ambrose put it, "white folks and negroes all come from one father" because "except the black skin, and the curled head, their bodies . . . are just alike, within and without," and "they are more alike in their souls, than in their bodies." Moral equality meant that masters owed the duty to their slaves to "require nothing but what is reasonable." As Wyatt-Brown observed, "there was always honor in *caritas,* the pre-Christian idea that the exercise of mercy honored the bestower," and "Christian benevolence reinforced the policy."

Law, according to the minister Ambrose quotes, could actually interfere with the moral demands on masters. Brutal masters were "known over a whole county." Their slaves would flee from them. The slaves might die or, if recaptured, be executed. Many Southern jurisdictions compensated masters for the value of slaves who were executed. This, the minister wrote, was wrong: Such laws might lead "some masters . . . to breed them less virtuously; and rather promote than discourage their [that is, the masters'] villainies." "Were it not so, some more care would have been taken, to instill virtuous, if not religious principles into these poor neglected creatures." Both masters and slaves, that is, were fallen human beings, tempted to misbehave; as Genovese suggested, no master who listened in church could really believe that he alone was a saint. Sometimes the law might impede the moral instruction that would bring masters and slaves alike closer to fulfilling their duties to God.

Ambrose's treatment of the law's relation to religion and moral reform focuses on the special statutes compensating masters. In economic terms such statutes create *moral hazard*: They increase the likelihood of misconduct by masters by compensating them for loss without regard to the masters' misconduct. (Some compensation statutes took moral hazard into account by reducing the compensation when specific circumstances indicated the master's partial responsibility for the slave's actions.) But the minister's emphasis on human sinfulness, like Weld's arguments discussed above, suggests a broader view of moral hazard. Religious leaders and their congregants, themselves subject to the temptation to forgo what they knew was right, might take the task of moral instruction less seriously if they knew that the law, rather than religion, was available to discipline slaveowners who demanded more than what was "reasonable" of their slaves and then punished the slaves for resisting the unreasonable demands. Law might thereby interfere with religion in promoting a good social order. And yet human sinfulness meant that no human institution would operate perfectly. In particular, Ambrose suggests, Southern churchmen understood that moral instruction would inevitably fall short and would have to be supplemented by legal sanctions, at least in extreme cases. As Ambrose puts it in an analysis of late antebellum defenses of slavery, slavery "had to be transformed so that it concurred with God's will," with individual slaveowners subject to state control pursuant to God's will.

To summarize: Judge Ruffin defended the proposition that the slaveowner's *legal* dominion had to be absolute. He acknowledged that this meant that the institutions of law would be unavailable to discipline slaveowners who misbehaved. He argued that making those institutions unavailable was necessary to ensure that slaves knew that they could not appeal for redress against their owners' misconduct. But, Ruffin argued, *other* institutions were available that reduced, and would continue to reduce, the possibility that slaveowners would actually mistreat their slaves. Yet Ruffin's argument was flawed in several ways. Deploying the other institutions sometimes raised the very risk of slaves' appealing to the community against their masters. And, perhaps more important, none of the institutions could guarantee that slaveowners would not misbehave. The law, perhaps, should have been available to supplement the other institutions for those cases, which Judge Ruffin may have believed to be few, where self-interest, honor, and religion failed to control the masters. In Genovese's summary, Southern slaveowners "erected a legal system the implications of which should have embarrassed them and sometimes did; and then they tried to hold it as a reserve. . . . The slave laws existed as a moral guide and an instrument for emergency use." Judge Ruffin's opinion in

State v. Mann exposed these tensions but did not diffuse them as the opinion asserted.

———

The Ambivalences of *State v. Mann*

One theme recurs in historians' studies of Southern law, Southern honor, and Southern religion. In each area, we find that claims made to sustain the power of the South's slaveowners were two-edged swords. Southern legal processes had to be fair if they were to claim the mantle of law, but fair processes sometimes undermined the masters' absolute dominion. For Wyatt-Brown, "the legal apparatus functioned to mediate between rich and poor, usually to the benefit of property holders but not so much as to put at a permanent risk the credibility of justice itself." With respect to religion, Genovese points out, "Christianity . . . preached the dignity and worth of the individual and therefore threatened to stimulate defiance to authority, even as it preached submission." For Wyatt-Brown, the honorable slaveowner was simultaneously, and intractably, independent of the community, exercising the "unchecked freedom to be one's own final authority," and dependent upon the community as the mirror in which honor was reflected. Genovese treats the two-edged characteristic of these institutions under the heading of *hegemony*.

The Italian Marxist Antonio Gramsci developed the concept of hegemony to account for what he regarded as a puzzle: the apparent agreement of the European working class to political arrangements that perpetuated their class position, when socialist parties were offering political platforms that promised a change in class relations. A ruling class can maintain its power by physical force, but, according to Gramsci, maintaining power through hegemony is better, because doing so places the ruling class at a lower risk of violent retaliation and because, at least in some cultures at some times, the routine deployment of physical force is inconsistent with deeply felt moral views among the ruling class itself.

Hegemony operates by persuasion rather than coercion: The ruling class offers arguments that it deserves its privileged status and subordinated classes deserve theirs. The arguments will of course differ from culture to culture. Sometimes the ruling class asserts that it deserves its position because it has received the blessing of God. Sometimes it does so on the ground that its members are better at organizing a society to provide material wealth than are members of the subordinated classes. Of course, whether these arguments are persuasive depends on many things. In the first society, for example, subordinated classes must believe both that receiving the blessing of God is actually something that could validate a ruling class's position and that the ruling class has received that blessing. In the second, they must believe both that the ruling class is better at providing material wealth and that organizing society to provide material wealth is what fundamentally matters.

According to Genovese, the law in the slave South "constituted a principal vehicle for the hegemony of the ruling class." As Genovese puts it, "The law acts hegemonically to assure people that their particular consciences can be subordinated—indeed, morally must be subordinated—to the collective judgment of society." For present purposes, Genovese can be said to identify three targets of law as that vehicle: elements of the ruling class itself, non-slaveholding whites, and the slaves. Within the slaveholding class, "[t]he most advanced fraction—those who most clearly perceived the interests and needs of the class as a whole— steadily worked to make their class more conscious of its nature, spirit, and destiny." For its project of bringing the ruling class as a whole "to a higher understanding of itself," the leading fraction used the law. But, according to Genovese, in guiding the slaveholding class, law had to "manifest a degree of evenhandedness sufficient to compel social conformity" and "validate itself ethically in the eyes of the several classes, not just the ruling class."

These are strong claims about how law must be structured if it is to be a principal vehicle, along with other institutions, in maintaining hegemony. The deepest claim is that law somehow communicates something about the moral order it defends to some audiences. Judicial opinions do provide arguments of the sort required in the theory of hegemony. But it is unclear to whom the opinions are directed. And in the case of *State v. Mann* the assertions that the legal rule the case announces is "harsh" and should be repudiated as "a principle of moral right" by "every man in his retirement" put into question how the opinion could "validate ethically" the rule to *any* audience. For Genovese, the legal system contributes to hegemony by identifying "standards of decency . . . in a world inhabited, like most worlds, by men who strove to be considered decent." *State v. Mann* seems to revel in the law's *indecency* when considered in moral terms. How might it contribute to hegemony nonetheless?

Judge Ruffin's opinion speaks to several audiences. Some passages seem to speak to Northerners unsympathetic to slavery. So, for example, Ruffin might be anticipating an adverse reaction by slavery's opponents in the North to the harsh rule he is about to announce when the opinion's second sentence cautions, "It is impossible that the reasons on which they go can be appreciated, but where institutions similar to our own exist and are thoroughly understood." Here Ruffin seems to say to hostile Northern readers that their hostility rests on ignorance. Near the opinion's conclusion, Ruffin refers to "a judiciary tainted with a false and fanatical philanthropy, seeking to redress an acknowledged evil by means still more wicked and appalling than even that evil." Plainly this cannot refer to Ruffin's own court, and it seems to refer instead to judges unfamiliar with slavery, that is, Northern judges.

These same phrases, however, speak to Southerners as well. The opinion's second sentence serves to damp down concern among Southern readers that the case's result will show that slavery is immoral, by including them within the circle of the knowledgeable who are able to appreciate the reasons for the decision. Genovese's emphasis on differences between leading fractions of the ruling class and less sophisticated elements helps us understand to whom Ruffin addressed his opinion. Ruffin is concerned about the "person in his retirement" who "must repudiate" the rule of absolute power "as a principle of moral right." Such a person has unreflectively absorbed teachings of moral principle without considering whether those principles should be applied as legal rules in "the state of slavery." The opinion seeks to educate such readers about "the actual condition of things." After they consider Judge Ruffin's arguments, they will be persuaded that, despite appearances and their moral prejudices, the legal rule announced makes sense, is just, and preserves slavery. The opinion, that is, aims to develop a hegemonic ideology *within* the slave-owning class. As legal historian Ariela Gross points out, maintaining hegemony "take[s] work." Judge Ruffin's opinion in *State v. Mann* was an example of the work of constructing hegemony.

Genovese also points out that hegemonic ideologies need to speak to the subordinated classes as well, and much of *Roll, Jordan, Roll* is devoted to an explication of the tensions when slaves adopted a Christian ideology that simultaneously valorized their individual self-worth as children of God and taught the importance of submission to higher authority. It is unlikely in the extreme that Judge Ruffin saw his opinion in *State v. Mann* as addressed directly to slaves. Southern law typically prohibited masters from educating their slaves, though many masters did anyway—perhaps another example of how Southern ideology embedded some rules in law while allowing other institutions to operate according to different standards. Nor, according to Ruffin himself, could slaves be expected to approve of the rule, at least as a moral principle: "What moral considerations shall be addressed to such a being to convince him what it is impossible but that the most stupid must feel and know can never be true—that he is thus to labor upon a principle of natural duty."

Still, slaves might learn *of* the decision. Ruffin's opinion might be taken as counseling them to take a posture of resigned acceptance. Even that, however, created a tension within Ruffin's opinion, for he wrote that a slave's "services can only be expected from one who has no will of his own; who surrenders his will in implicit obedience to that of another." *Acceptance* entails choice, that is, the exercise of will. And, indeed, every Southerner who gave serious thought to slavery knew, and acknowledged, that slaves did have wills of their own.

The law treated slaves as persons with the capacity to choose. Slaves could be held liable for their criminal acts, for example. A slave's hirer might not be liable to the slave's owner when the slave was injured due to the slave's own choices. The acknowledgment of the slave's will, contrary to Ruffin's assertion, was extremely important. In Genovese's words, it "exposed . . . the notion that in fact, not merely in one's fantasy life, some human beings could become mere extensions of the will of another. . . . [E]ven one right, imperfectly defended, was enough to tell them that the pretensions of the master class could be resisted." Genovese writes that "the slaves as well as the masters were creating the law." Walter Johnson and Ariela Gross have shown how slaves did so. Johnson shows how slaves placed on sale presented themselves in ways that made them attractive or unattractive to particular buyers: "By knowing what slaveholders were looking for, slaves could turn their own commodification against their enslavement." Gross examines the performances occurring in Southern courtrooms when witnesses testified about slaves and demonstrates that those performances were exercises in constructing hegemony. Witnesses offered interpretations of slaves' conduct, cast as description, in terms that comported with the witnesses' understanding of how slaves *should* behave. They exercised their moral agency to construct the stories that were presented in litigation where the slaves were nominally only objects. For slaves as moral actors, *State v. Mann* could not possibly serve the law's hegemonic goals.

How, then, did *State v. Mann* follow "the logic of slavery," as Genovese says? Abolitionist writers agreed that *State v. Mann* captured the essence of slavery, seeing in the decision a pure argument that slavery required the absolute dominion of master over slave. Abolitionist writers agreed, as well, that absolute dominion was morally repugnant. For them, Judge Ruffin's opinion demonstrated, and embraced, the immorality of slavery.

There are obvious problems with this reading of the logic of slavery as exposed in *Mann*. Judge Ruffin plainly did not think that slavery was immoral, even though he believed that absolute dominion was indeed morally repugnant. Judge Ruffin's opinion pursued a strategy of institutional allocation: The law had to be immunized from "general reasoning" and had to defend the master's absolute *legal* dominion over his slaves, while allowing moral considerations to shape masters' behavior through other institutions such as the code of honor and religion.

Seeing *State v. Mann* as a case about institutions rather than one about substantive rules regulating masters' behavior casts the phrase "the logic of slavery" in a somewhat different light. Judge Ruffin constructed his opinion as a *description* of "the state of slavery." For Ruffin, the proposition that "[t]he power of the master must be absolute to render the submission of the slave perfect" was, descriptively, "inherent in the relation of master and slave." On this reading, the opinion in *State v. Mann* works out the logic of slavery by exposing the presuppositions inherent in the system.

Notably, the logic of slavery need not correspond to slavery as it was actually practiced when Judge Ruffin wrote. So, for example, widespread practices of slave trading and particularly the breakup of families when slaves were sold might be thought inconsistent with Judge Ruffin's references to the close relations between masters and their slaves as one reason for thinking that it was unnecessary to make masters criminally liable for abusing their slaves. As historian Walter Johnson argues, the events surrounding slave sales no less than the events occurring during the master-slave relationship were important sources of the psychological constructs that slaveowners used to understand slavery. Even so, Judge Ruffin's description of the logic of slavery might be accurate in some sense. Many sales of slaves occurred in connection with winding up estates after a master died. Though the initial owner might have had the kinds of relations with his slaves that Judge Ruffin described, the heirs might not—but the new purchasers might develop those relations. In addition, slave traders were widely regarded among slaveowners as morally questionable characters, indicating that slave sales, while common, might nonetheless be inconsistent with the "logic" of slavery.

Judge Ruffin's exposition of the logic of slavery might best be understood as an attempt to describe what slavery would be like were it allowed to develop unimpeded. Slave sales might be rare and family breakups unknown in the mature state of slavery implied by Judge Ruffin's logic, for example. Of course, slavery did not develop without interference. The Civil War ended slavery, but perhaps even more important for understanding the limits of Judge Ruffin's argument, slaveowners were deeply implicated in a system of market-based exchanges—of the products slaves helped produce—that had a different logic from the one Judge Ruffin described. A full account of the logic of the actual system of Southern slavery would have had to reconcile what Judge Ruffin said about the logic of slavery with the dynamics of market exchanges. It is not clear what such a reconciliation would look like, or whether one was even possible. Neither Judge Ruffin nor any other Southern jurist attempted the task.

Alternatively, Judge Ruffin might have been attempting to persuade his audiences that Southern society *ought* to move in the direction of a sharp separation of the institutions for shaping masters' behavior. On this reading, his opinion was an attempt to *construct* a slave society organized, as he saw it, according to the institutional logic of slavery.

If the logic of slavery is absolute legal dominion and community control of masters through nonlegal institutions, *State v. Mann* does develop the logic of slavery better than any other opinion in the slave South.

CHAPTER 4

Places and Persons

So far I have examined Judge Ruffin's opinion in *State v. Mann*, taking it as a document standing alone. But of course the opinion came from somewhere—in two senses. The case of *State v. Mann* came from a local court in Chowan County, North Carolina, and the opinion came from Judge Ruffin, a newly appointed judge seeking to enhance his reputation. This chapter examines what can be known about both sources of *State v. Mann*.

The Case

Legal historian Sally Hadden says that *State v. Mann* began "with a horrific confrontation." Judge Ruffin's rhetoric certainly suggests that something quite awful had happened. His "lament" about "such cases as these" and his desire to avoid "this ungrateful question" would be disproportionate unless the decision relieved from liability someone who had done something dramatically wrong.

Judge Ruffin may have known more than the surviving historical records show, but today we know—and seemingly can know—very little about the events that precipitated *State v. Mann*. Historians have written micro-histories of previously obscure legal cases when they have discovered archives containing documents whose careful examination allows exploration of a wide range of issues connected to the cases. Historians have also written histories of famous cases by working backward, examining trial records, newspaper accounts, and personal and organizational records to illuminate the social and political context out of which the cases arose. *State v. Mann* is a famous case, but very little survives from which a historian can re-create its background. Most trial records of North Carolina slave cases were destroyed during the Civil War. The record on appeal in *State v. Mann* does exist, but it contains little from which more information can be teased out. Basically, what we can *know* about the events underlying *State v. Mann* is contained in Judge Ruffin's opinion.

Still, it is possible to make some educated guesses about the case. In particular, although it is impossible to be sure, John Mann's assault on Lydia may well have been, as assaults involving gunshot wounds go, a relatively mild rather than a horrific confrontation.

Convicted of assault, John Mann was fined five dollars (a figure that does not appear in Judge Ruffin's opinion). How much was that? Calculations based on cost-of-living estimates that are conceded to be inexact indicate that a five-dollar fine in 1828 would be a fine of about ninety dollars today. We would regard someone who was fined ninety dollars today for assaulting another person as having received a slap on the wrist.

Issues of the newspaper published in 1827 and 1828 in Edenton, the county seat where Mann was prosecuted, provide additional clues as to the seriousness of the punishment Mann received, and so, indirectly, of the seriousness of his offense. In 1827 a subscription to the newspaper was three dollars. In the same year, a reward of ten dollars was offered for a runaway male slave and a reward of five dollars for a runaway female slave, and in 1828 rewards of ten dollars for a male aged forty to forty-five and a male who was eighteen or nineteen years old. Other rewards were larger: forty dollars for two runaway women, fifty dollars the next year for a male. These figures are unfortunately ambiguous. Five dollars, a little more than the price of a newspaper subscription, does not seem like a lot of money, and yet rewards for runaway slaves were sometimes not that much more, suggesting that five or ten dollars might be close to the full value of a slave, at least one who was rebellious enough to run away—or, perhaps, as with Lydia, rebellious enough to resist punishment.

The surviving issues of the local newspaper, which was published from 1826 to 1831, deal primarily with events occurring in the state capital or in Washington. There is a long gap in surviving issues for the months in 1828 when Mann probably assaulted Lydia, and local events were rarely reported in issues that are available. In 1827, the newspaper did report a "disgusting occurrence," involving the death of a young slave in the course of punishment for "some offense." The slave, in his early teens, was told to stand on a stool with a noose around his neck for a few hours one morning. At some point the slave fell or jumped off the stool and died. (The newspaper did not suggest that he had been pushed off the stool.) But the fact that no newspaper accounts of Mann's offense can be found carries little weight.

One fairly extensive report does exist regarding slave abuse in the years surrounding *State v. Mann* in the area where the case occurred, but nothing like the facts of *State v. Mann* appears in the report. That, however, is again no more than suggestive. The report is the well-known autobiography of Harriet Ann Jacobs, which was published in 1861 as *Incidents in the Life of a Slave Girl*, with the author's name concealed by the pseudonym Linda Brent and many events similarly cloaked with false names. Recent research, though, has identified the people Jacobs wrote about and has confirmed the accuracy of her account.

Jacobs was born in Edenton in 1813. Her mistress took her into the family home when Harriet's mother died in 1819. The mistress died in 1825, and Jacobs became the property of a three-year-old child and moved to the child's home. There the child's father, Dr. James Norcom, began to harass Jacobs sexually, and Mrs. Norcom responded with jealous abuse. Jacobs began a sexual relationship with a neighbor in 1829 and soon had two children with him. Norcom reacted by sending Jacobs to a plantation where she would work as a field hand rather than as a more privileged house slave. Jacobs ran away and went into hiding in the attic of the house owned by her grandmother, a former slave. She lived in the attic for seven years, and in 1842 Jacobs escaped from Edenton. Eventually she became active in antislavery circles. At the urging of Lydia Maria Child, a noted feminist and abolitionist, Jacobs wrote her autobiography and published it in 1861.

Jacobs's book tells a gruesome tale of sexual and physical abuse. At Child's urging, Jacobs supplemented her personal story with a chapter of "Sketches of Neighboring Slaveholders," designed to show that Jacobs's story, while unique in its details, was also representative of slavery. Jacobs describes five abusive slave-owners. One owned a large plantation with "a jail and a whipping post." His brother had "well trained" bloodhounds who tore a runaway to death. A neighbor of these two was offended, while drunk, by a servant; he had the man stripped and exposed to elements during a stormy winter night. Another neighbor was a woman who "lashed her slaves with the might of a man." Finally, Jacobs describes a childhood friend who was taken by her owner to Louisiana, where she had a son who was later murdered by a new owner.

None of these sketches describes an incident like that in *State v. Mann*. Jacobs's modern editor, Jean Fagan Yellin, confirmed many of the facts in the book, but Yellin notes that the chapter of sketches "does not appear correct in its details," although Jacobs's account of the violence committed by the two brothers "is substantially accurate." She notes that in 1816 the plantation owner was charged with beating a slave and assaulting two white men, was convicted of assault and battery with intent to commit murder, and was fined four hundred dollars (although it is unclear whether the fine related to the assaults on the white men or the assault on the slave).

Yellin points out that Jacobs "was a townswoman generally unacquainted with the countryside" and that "it was and is inherently difficult to document atrocities against slaves." One might have expected Child to press Jacobs to include as much as Jacobs could about "horrific" assaults on slaves. The notoriety of *State v. Mann* and the fact that it arose in Edenton's county while Jacobs lived there suggest that Child at least would have found it valuable to include Jacobs's rendition of the facts in her book—if those facts conformed to the image of slavery that Jacobs conveyed. Still, the most that can be drawn from the absence of *State v. Mann* from Jacobs's account is the simple observation that she did not include it, either because she did not know of it, because it was less awful than the few sketches she did provide, or because it was not as bad as Judge Ruffin's language suggested.

Finally, there is the conviction itself. Mann's jury was drawn from the town of Edenton, Chowan County's center, and the countryside. Most jurors were slaveowners themselves, some with relatively small holdings as revealed in the 1820 and 1830 census reports (one owned a single slave, others four and seven), others with relatively large holdings (from fourteen to forty-four and seventy-six). The ambiguities of census data are suggested by the reports from 1820 and 1830 about Thomas Brownrigg, who seems to have headed a household of seven whites and five slaves in 1820, and then appears to have been the only white in a household with twenty-six slaves in 1830. Another, Joseph H. Skinner, was probably a member of a family whose earlier investments had helped revitalize Chowan County's fishing industry. It is probably fair to say that Mann's jury was a cross section of Chowan County's adult white male population.

Jacobs's story hints that Chowan County juries might have been particularly sympathetic to claims that slaves had been abused. Her modern editor found that one of the men she described had been charged with assaulting a slave in 1819, when he whipped and cut her with a knife. The defendant moved for a change of venue, alleging that he could not get a fair trial in Chowan County. After the trial was moved, the defendant was acquitted. Again, however, the evidence about jury sentiment in Chowan County turns out to be ambiguous: In 1820 a grand jury refused to indict the same person when a slave woman was found beaten to death in his house.

What can we discover about Lydia's owner? The 1830 census reports three Jones families in Chowan County, including one headed by "Liza" (not Elizabeth) Jones. None of the families owned slaves, though. Liza, whose age was between thirty and fifty, headed a household with four children and one man in the same age range as Liza. John Jones, in his twenties, headed a household with three women roughly his age and one older woman, probably his mother. We cannot know whether either of these families had owned Lydia in 1828 but had sold her by the time of the 1830 census. If they had, she would have been one of a very few slaves at most in the household.

That, in turn, might help us understand John Mann. In 1830 someone named John Mann was living in Chowan County, in a household with two men, one in his thirties and one in his forties. Slave hiring fell into two patterns, one involving the hiring of slaves for plantation work and the other involving their hiring for domestic work. Keith Barton, examining slave hiring in a Kentucky plantation county a few decades after *State v. Mann*, found that most hirers were people with limited financial resources who hired a single slave. And most of the slaves who were hired were, like Lydia, women. According to Barton, "These women were hired almost exclusively to perform domestic tasks such as laundry, cooking, and child care." The fact, if it be so, that John Mann was not married suggests that he might have had a particular need for a slave to use for the first two of those purposes.

Finally, the fact—again, if it be so—that John Mann was living in relative isolation in 1830 suggests that he might have been socially isolated *because of* his assault on Lydia—and, we might think, socially isolated even before that, perhaps because he had a bad reputation. Mann's possible social isolation might account for the willingness of a jury composed of respectable slaveowners to convict him of assaulting a slave. It may also suggest a reason for a *criminal* prosecution rather than a civil action by Elizabeth Jones: Mann may fit the economists' model of a slave hirer who lacked the resources to compensate the hired slave's owner for damages he inflicted.

In sum, we can discover few of the facts underlying *State v. Mann*. John Mann's assault on Lydia may have been "horrific," as the conviction itself suggests, or it may have been relatively minor, as the size of the fine suggests. His conviction suggests that he may have been socially isolated in Edenton and that Elizabeth Jones may have been a person of relatively high standing whose loss, small or large, the prosecutor and the jury's members thought deserved to be acknowledged. Judge Ruffin's rhetoric may have been well chosen no matter what the facts, for, as one scholar reminds us in writing about slavery's depiction in literature, the effectiveness of violence may sometimes be "indicated precisely by its invisibility or transparency."

The Setting

Chowan County lies at the end of Albemarle Sound, and it was one of the earliest settled sites in the state. For many years Edenton was the colony's informal capital. It was the hometown of U.S. Supreme Court Justice James Iredell and the place of death of U.S. Supreme Court Justice James Wilson, one of the major participants in the Constitution's drafting and ratification debates. Edenton became a major port city, a "place of great wealth" according to a local historian. It was a center for the export of lumber and its derivatives, important in the construction of oceangoing ships, and a center as well for the cotton trade. In the early 1800s Edenton was the home of the largest rope-making enterprise in the United States. The city suffered economic reverses during the War of 1812, though growth resumed afterward. True economic decline set in a decade after *State v. Mann*, with the depression of 1837 and the construction of a canal through the Great Dismal Swamp, which shifted much of the city's trade to Norfolk, Virginia. Chowan County's population in 1820 was about 6,400; it declined to barely 1,000 by 1860.

Chowan County produced cotton and tobacco, with over three-quarters of its population in the 1820s living in the countryside. The county had a slight majority of slaves—in 1820, approximately 3,400 slaves and 2,800 whites, a disparity that persisted until the Civil War. In the 1820s more than 130 free persons of color lived in the county, divided evenly between Edenton and the countryside, and 50 of the free colored population actually voted in 1834.

North Carolina had experienced an "explosive growth" of its free black population in the first decades of the nineteenth century. According to Hadden, "many rumors circulated at the end of the 1820s" about the possibility that free blacks would gain political power and help free all the slaves, and more specifically about possible slave rebellions. In 1826 the state legislature prohibited the migration of free blacks into the state and authorized sentences of up to three years' servitude for free blacks already in the state who were "idle" or "dissipated." Some slaveowners in North Carolina were familiar with discussions in Virginia about revising that state's constitution, which non-slaveholders in western Virginia correctly believed favored the slaveowners of eastern Virginia. As Hadden puts it, "whites and blacks were on edge at the end of 1829," anxious about political developments and the possibility of slave rebellion.

Hadden points out that that anxiety was fueled by the September 1829 publication in Boston of David Walker's *Appeal . . . to the Coloured Citizens of the World.* The *Appeal* reached Georgia in December 1829 and was available in Virginia a week or two later. The *Appeal* was one of the first widely circulated denunciations of slavery written by an African American. Slaveowners regarded Walker's language as inflammatory. Walker described whites as "an unjust, jealous, unmerciful, avaricious and blood-thirsty set of beings, always seeking after power and authority." He continued, in what was generally and probably correctly taken as a threat of rebellion, "unless you speedily alter your course, *you* and your *Country are gone!!!!*" Walker's statement that slaveowners were "the Lord's enemies" and should "be destroyed" could be taken as a metaphor or a call for the extinction of slaveowners by means of the extinction of slavery, but the more natural reading was the literal one, that Walker was urging rebellion. Walker addressed his black readers: "Oh! my coloured brethren, all over the world, when shall we arise from this death-like apathy?—And be men!!" Walker expressed his commitment strongly: "I count my life not dear unto me, but I am ready to be offered at any moment, For what is the use of living, when in fact I am dead."

Walker's *Appeal* did not arrive in North Carolina until after *State v. Mann* was decided, but Hadden argues that Judge Ruffin probably knew of the *Appeal*'s existence and content from his cousin Thomas Ritchie, the editor of a Virginia newspaper to which Ruffin subscribed. The newspaper published an editorial denouncing the *Appeal* at the end of January 1830, just two weeks before the North Carolina Supreme Court took up Mann's appeal of his conviction. Ruffin's specific knowledge of the *Appeal* may be less important than Hadden's more general point: While antislavery agitation had not become widespread by 1830, slave-owners may have already understood, from rumors confirmed by documents like the *Appeal*, that defenders of slavery needed to articulate—for themselves, and for their opponents—the grounds on which slavery rested. Hadden argues that *State v. Mann* is best understood against this background of emerging nervousness about slavery's survival.

Hadden's argument is supported by events in Chowan County in September 1831, a little more than a year after *State v. Mann* was decided. In late August 1831, the news of Nat Turner's rebellion in Southampton, Virginia, reached Chowan County. According to the county's historian, the news "set off waves of panic" in the area. Whites organized a thorough search of the Great Dismal Swamp, and "[b]y the end of the first week of September nineteen stray Negroes had been rounded up and placed in Edenton jail." The pump had to have been primed for such a reaction to occur, and the priming probably was a process that extended backward to the period when Judge Ruffin was writing *State v. Mann*.

———

Becoming a Judge: Ruffin's Jurisprudence

In lectures delivered in 1936, longtime Harvard Law School dean Roscoe Pound listed Thomas Ruffin as one of the finest common law judges in U.S. history. Pound did not spell out his criteria explicitly, but his lectures make them reasonably clear. Pound praised "the judicial search for the workable legal precept, for the principle which is fruitful of good results in giving satisfactory grounds of decisions of actual cases." He offered three criteria for identifying the great judges whose searches were regularly successful: reasoned application of the law the judges receive from a tradition; responsiveness to the need to adapt the law to new circumstances; and attention to the role of judicial decisions as precedent.

Pound's exposition intertwines the first two of these criteria. Great judges, in Pound's view, "work[ed] out from our inherited legal material a general body of law for what was to be a politically and economically unified land." Such judges continued "the taught legal tradition," and developed "new reasoned applications of the technique in which [they] . . . had been trained to the body of legal precepts and established legal analogies which had been taught them." For Pound, "Reason is applied to experience to work out adjustments of relations under new conditions." These "reasoned applications" responded to "new demands, problems created by the development of transportation, the effect of inventions, and the rise of industry in some sections and growth of trade in others." The "taught tradition" came to "serve new purposes as old doctrines were called upon to solve new problems." In this way, Pound wrote, "strong judge[s] . . . knew how to use the precepts of the law to advance justice in the concrete case."

Pound required something more of great judges. Their decisions had to work as precedents: The decisions had to "serve, first, as a measure or pattern of decision of like cases for the future, and, second, as a basis for analogical reasoning in the future for cases for which no exact precedents are at hand." The role of precedent sometimes required judges to resist "the appealing circumstances of one case," in the process "sacrific[ing] . . . the claims of particular litigants."

Pound explained his points by referring to developments in the law of accidents, produced by the expansion of railroads, and the law of labor relations, produced by industrial development. Obviously *State v. Mann* does not fit within any of these categories, nor would we say that the result advanced justice. Still, we might be able to read Judge Ruffin's opinion with Pound's criteria in mind, particularly if we are willing to concede to Ruffin his view that slavery was not unjust.

Born in Virginia in 1787, Ruffin attended Princeton University and then read law back in Virginia. Joining the rest of his family, he moved to North Carolina in 1807, where he continued to study law with "a daring, sometimes scheming, intellectual," according to historian Timothy Huebner. Ruffin's mentor Archibald Murphey promoted educational change through the creation of public schools and economic development through the building of canals and roads. Ruffin was admitted to the bar in 1808 and quickly moved into politics, serving as a member of North Carolina's lower house from 1813 to 1816, ending up as speaker of the house. As Huebner says, Ruffin "stepped in and out of the political arena his entire career."

Ruffin resigned from the house to become a judge in 1816 and served for two years on the state's trial bench. After practicing law for seven years, during which he trained a large number of students who read law with him, Ruffin returned to the trial bench in 1825, where he served for three more years before resigning to become president of North Carolina's state bank. In 1829 the governor and state council chose Ruffin for the state supreme court. *State v. Mann*, decided in January 1830, was one of Judge Ruffin's first opinions as an appellate judge.

Assessing *State v. Mann*'s place in Judge Ruffin's jurisprudence requires attention to some of his other important decisions, although it may be worth noting that a decision rendered relatively early in a judge's career may not express everything present in the judge's mature jurisprudence. Ruffin wrote hundreds of opinions in his decades on the bench, and it probably would be easy to find cases that would illustrate almost any conceivable characterization of Ruffin's jurisprudence. J. G. de Roulhac Hamilton, who compiled Ruffin's papers for the North Carolina Historical Commission, included five cases in the published version of the papers, presumably deeming them the most important or illuminating in the corpus. One was *State v. Mann*. The others do indeed illuminate Ruffin's jurisprudence quite well. Here it will be sufficient to consider only two of these cases; one of the others is important largely for its political significance, and the other is too technical to warrant extended consideration here.

Wiswall v. Brinson (1850) is a dazzling example of Ruffin's facility in case distinguishing. Hiron Brinson wanted a house moved from one location to another about two hundred yards away. He hired Gaskill to do the work. Brinson did not supervise the operation, although he did watch as Gaskill directed the moving. To assist in moving the house, Gaskill drilled a hole in the middle of the street and then forgot to refill it. The next night, Howell Wiswall was driving a carriage down the street when one of the horses stepped into the hole and was injured. Wiswall sued Brinson, on the theory that Brinson should be liable for the concededly negligent acts of the person he hired.

A majority of the North Carolina Supreme Court agreed with Wiswall, but Judge Ruffin dissented. Ruffin's analytic difficulty was that there was a large body of case law establishing that a homeowner was liable for damages caused by negligence of his employees, including contractors, *in the home itself.* But, he argued, none of the cases involved negligence that occurred *outside* the home, as it had here. Some cases involved negligence in connection with building materials left outside the home, but on the defendant's land. Ruffin thus read the case law as dealing with *property* law, the law relating to an owner's responsibility for what happened on his own land, rather than dealing with tort law, the general law of responsibility for accidents. Because the accident here did not occur on Brinson's land, the cases were irrelevant.

What is remarkable is that *every* case Ruffin discussed actually ended up imposing liability on the defendant. But, as a strong judge of the sort Pound admired, Ruffin offered a justification for his reading of the cases: They "show[ed] negatively, but conclusively, that the defendant [in this case] is not liable." Ruffin used the cases to develop a principle of potential control. When a homeowner hired a contractor to do work on the premises, the homeowner was in a position to supervise the contractor's operations. But, Ruffin argued, it would be unreasonable to think the homeowner could control everything the contractor did, and especially not what the contractor did off the premises. Ruffin posed a hypothetical case: Suppose the contractor went miles away to purchase lumber for the repair, and then injured someone while driving back to the house. Surely the homeowner should not be liable for the contractor's ordinary negligence.

After all, "[b]y no possibility can one be at all those places where all the persons whom one may be under the necessity of employing about personal matter may happen from time to time to be, so as to correct their misdoings."

Ruffin then turned to the law of master and servant, which had a well-established rule that an employer was liable for the negligent acts of his employees. *Wiswall*'s most enduring contribution to the law was Judge Ruffin's analysis of when one person was the employee of another rather than an independent contractor. The rule imposing liability on employers required that an employment relationship exist. It could not be, Ruffin wrote, that the mere "procuring of work to be done for one by another creates that relation." Employees were one thing, independent contractors such as Gaskill another. We can determine whether someone is an employee or an independent contractor by examining "whether the person employed is subject to the orders and control of the employer." Ruffin noted that the entire line of cases he had previously discussed as property cases would have been easily decided as master-servant cases, if the courts had treated independent contractors as servants. He then went through another set of cases to show that they distinguished between employees and contractors precisely on the ground of the employer's control, although he conceded that some of the cases "turn[ed] upon very nice points, as to the facts from which it was inferred that the employer had or had not the control of a person actually working for him."

The second case to consider here is *Raleigh and Gaston Railroad v. Davis* (1837), which validated North Carolina's program of public support for railroad development and was, according to Huebner, one of two antebellum decisions that were "seminal in the development of American railroad law." The state legislature gave the railroad company a charter and authorized it to take a landowner's property for construction of the line. The railroad had to pay, of course, but if it could not reach an agreement with the landowner, the statute provided for the amount to be set by a panel of five disinterested property owners. Richard Davis owned land over which the railroad would run. He objected to the entire proceeding, asserting that the statute violated his right to property and his right to a jury trial. Judge Ruffin, writing for a unanimous court, upheld the statute.

The opinion opened by finding it "universally acknowledged" that the public had a right to take private property "to the extent that the use of it is needful and advantageous to the public." This power was "useful and necessary to every body politic." The North Carolina state legislature could exercise this sovereign power even though the state's constitution did not specifically list it—as it omitted the power to tax or dispose of vacant lands. The legislature's power of eminent domain, according to Judge Ruffin, is "founded on necessity," but "it is a necessity that varies in urgency" depending on how the state might develop. This implied that the legislature had substantial discretion in deciding how to exercise the power. In particular, although the opinion assumed that the constitution gave Richards a right to compensation because of "natural right and justice," "the sense of right and wrong varies so much . . . and the principles of natural justice are so uncertain, that they cannot be referred to as a sure standard of constitutional power." Only specific guarantees in the constitution provided such a standard, and Judge Ruffin found none requiring that a traditional jury determine the amount of compensation.

Davis's lawyer also objected to the fact that the railroad company could seize the land and then pay compensation, arguing that this would allow the railroad company to take land that really did not advance any public interest; requiring the courts to approve the seizure beforehand would guard against such abuses of power. Again, though, Ruffin was concerned about the proposed principle's application in other cases, writing, "[I]t seems impossible to lay it down as a principle, that compensation is indispensably a condition precedent," because "[t]he exigencies of the public may be too urgent to admit of . . . delay." Ruffin's example was wartime, but he also pointed to the need to get timber or stone to build the road, when no one could know in advance how much wood or rock would be needed.

Judge Ruffin bolstered his argument by pointing out that the rule he followed was the one developed in England under the

Magna Carta, a document held "in reverence" by U.S. courts and legislatures. Prior legislation in other states also provided "an authoritative exposition of the general sense through a long course of time, of the relative rights of the public and of individuals." The legislature had to provide some method of compensating owners for land taken for public uses, but it had discretion to decide how to figure out the amount to pay. The state constitution's preservation of "the ancient mode of trial by jury," he continued, "has a technical, peculiar, and well understood sense"; and Ruffin provided a number of examples to show that the constitutional guarantee did not cover a mere dispute over the amount of compensation for property taken for a public use.

The final question Ruffin addressed was in some ways the most important one. Davis's lawyer argued that his client was losing his property to a railroad company, not to the state government, and so "this taking is not legitimate, because the property is bestowed on private persons." Ruffin conceded that the corporation was a private one, "but it is constituted to effect a public benefit." In the past, the government owned all highways, but "[a]n immense and beneficial revolution has been brought about in modern times, by engaging individual enterprise, industry, and economy, in the execution of public works of internal improvement." Private individuals would develop the railroad, but under the legislature's general oversight. From the corporation's point of view, of course, the road was private (the corporation collected the fares and made the profits), but from the public's point of view the railroad was "a highway." He concluded, "[The land] is taken to be immediately and directly applied to an established public use, under the control and direction of the public authorities, with only such incidental private interests as the legislature has thought proper to admit, as the means of effecting the work and insuring a long preservation of it for the public use."

These two cases indicate why Pound thought Judge Ruffin a great common law judge. *Wiswall v. Brinson* is, from a technical point of view, a spectacular display of Ruffin's ability to work within the legal tradition by taking decided cases and extracting a general principle from them to guide judgment in a new case.

One might question whether the result was just, but no one reading the decision could doubt Ruffin's legal facility.

As Huebner points out in connection with the Davis case, Ruffin "focused less on the personal situation of an individual" than "on the implications of the court's decision[s]" for North Carolina's policy. The same might be said of *Wiswall*, where Judge Ruffin discounted the fact that the defendant actually was present while the contractor was moving his house and so, at least in theory, might have exercised some control over what the contractor did. Judge Ruffin was concerned with the *rule* the court adopted, not with individualized justice in the case before him. Ruffin's analysis of the master-servant cases suggested that mere presence might not be enough, because the defendant might not have known enough about how to move a house to be able to tell the contractor what to do. But the master-servant cases Ruffin described said that the relationship existed where the employer had a *right* to control, not where the employer had both the right to control and sufficient knowledge to control effectively. Had Ruffin been concerned about individualized justice, he would have had to do a bit more in analyzing the master-servant cases to explain why the defendant's lack of knowledge about how to move houses differed from other employers' lack of knowledge about the technical aspects of the work their employees did. Ruffin's careful analysis of the cases for other purposes shows that he certainly could have done the additional work; the fact that he did not indicates his indifference to individualized justice.

Davis was more focused on policy than on precedent, although Ruffin did draw effectively on prior cases to support his conclusion. More important, though, was Ruffin's reliance on the "revolution" in thinking about the role of individual enterprise in internal improvements. Here he showed how a legal rule could incorporate modern developments in the society and the economy, just as Pound's criteria required.

Huebner describes Judge Ruffin's jurisprudence in general terms as well. Huebner argues that Ruffin "conceived of his judicial role . . . as an extension of his political and policy-making endeavors" and took a pragmatic and flexible approach to crafting the law. *Davis*, for example, ruled in favor of development, which Ruffin himself valued "[a]s a banker and entrepreneur." Overall, according to Huebner, Judge Ruffin treated cases "not as controversies between individual litigants but as broad social and political conflicts."

In what is probably the most influential work in recent legal history, Morton Horwitz described a "transformation" of American law from a formalist, deductive approach to one that he called instrumental. For Horwitz, judges acting instrumentally used the law to promote public policies they believed important. They interpreted the precedents in light of the policies the precedents advanced—or in light of the policies the judges thought important.

Horwitz's instrumentalist judges were quite similar to Pound's great common law jurists, and it is no surprise that, although Horwitz did not discuss Ruffin's work, the cases we have examined are resoundingly instrumentalist. Concern for public policy is apparent on the surface of the railroad case. It is present in the house owner's liability case as well, although there Ruffin's dazzling deployment of the precedents obscures policy's role. Ruffin wanted to develop a legal rule that would allow entrepreneurial activity to go on unimpeded by fear of liability. Entrepreneurs might organize their businesses in a number of ways, one of which would involve extensive use of independent contractors. It was therefore important, for Ruffin, that the definition of employee be narrow enough to exclude independent contractors who might work far from the entrepreneur's direct supervision. That narrow definition is what he accomplished through his creative reading of apparently adverse precedents.

State v. Mann too expresses Judge Ruffin's practical and instrumentalist jurisprudence. In Huebner's words, the decision reflects "a cautious flexibility on his part—a preoccupation with weighing the social and political outcome of any decision involving slavery." Horwitz's work focuses on judges who developed rules facilitating capitalist enterprise, but there is no reason in principle to deny the instrumentalist label to Ruffin, who wrote explicitly about the policy bases for *State v. Mann*, where the policy was preserving slavery rather than expanding capitalism.

With respect to the taught legal tradition, two aspects of *State v. Mann* deserve note. First, tradition as such played an important role in validating the rule Ruffin articulated. Ruffin wrote that it had not "been hitherto contended" that masters could be liable for assaulting their slaves, and he noted that there had been no prosecutions "of this sort." Ruffin then wrote, "The established habits and uniform practice of the country in this respect is the best evidence of the portion of power deemed by the whole community requisite to the preservation of the master's dominion." Long-established practice thus provided strong support for the rule in *State v. Mann*, even if it might not be conclusive. Again adverting to the power of tradition as a basis for law independent of any policy evaluations, Ruffin continued, "If we thought differently we could not set our notions in array against the judgment of everybody else, and say that this or that authority may be safely lopped off."

Second, Judge Ruffin's discussion of the proposed analogy between slavery and "other domestic relations" worked within the taught tradition. That tradition required judges to produce, in Pound's terms, "reasoned" distinctions if they rejected the application of rules developed in one set of cases to the case at hand. Judge Ruffin did exactly that. He explained *why* "[t]here is no likeness between the cases." For Ruffin, the distinction could be found in the purposes of the rules applicable to other domestic relations. There the goal was "the happiness of the youth, born to equal rights with that of the governor." Given that goal, restricting the "governor"—the parent or apprentice's master—to "[m]oderate force" made sense because the governor could use "moral and intellectual instruction" to induce the youth to behave well. With slavery, though, the goal was not moral development of equals; there "[t]he end is the profit of the master, his security and the public safety." Moral instruction could not suffice to convince a slave that the master-slave relationship was in the slave's long-term interest. Only "uncontrolled authority over the body" could "produce this effect." Whatever one thinks of the morality of the distinction Ruffin draws, it clearly is an application of the legal tradition's insistence that adequate reasons be offered for treating cases differently.

Similarly, the analysis in Chapters 2 and 3 indicates how Judge Ruffin paid attention to the role of his decision as potential precedent. He refused to "enter upon a train of general reasoning" about the legality of masters' assaults on their slaves, because to do so would require courts in the future to "graduate the punishment appropriate to every temper and every dereliction of menial duty." The circumstances in which masters beat (or punished, or assaulted) their slaves were too varied to allow courts to shape a legal rule that would adequately respond to all the variations: "No man can anticipate the many and aggravated provocations of the master which the slave would be constantly stimulated by his own passions or the instigation of others to give." Further, Ruffin's statements of regret and his acknowledgment of the "harshness" of the rule in *State v. Mann* recall Huebner's analysis of the Davis railroad case. Like Ruffin's elevation of the public interest there over Davis's personal situation, his comments in *State v. Mann* can be understood as expressing Ruffin's understanding of the unavoidable tension between developing a sound rule of law and the "appealing circumstances of one case."

Little needs to be said explicitly about the role of policy concerns—"pragmatism" in some sense—in *State v. Mann*, because those concerns pervade the opinion. Perhaps more important, once again, is the way Judge Ruffin's approach to the law may have affected the opinion's rhetoric. Ruffin wanted to develop a legal rule that fit the necessities of slavery. Doing so meant ignoring the possibility that the legal rule might work a real injustice in an individual case even though it made more sense than any alternative for the great run of cases. So, for example, Ruffin conceded that "there may be particular instances of cruelty and deliberate barbarity where, in conscience, the law might properly interfere." The heightened rhetoric of the opinion suggests that Mann's case might indeed be one of those "particular instances." Even if it was not, Judge Ruffin's rhetoric certainly made it easy for readers, at the time and since, to assume that he was willing to ignore what he himself believed to be barbaric behavior in the service of a larger social goal, the preservation of slavery.

Seeing *State v. Mann* as an instrumentalist decision in Horwitz's sense casts some light on the moral-formal dilemma discussed in Chapter 3. For Robert Cover, judges confronted a moral-formal dilemma when they found themselves pulled in one direction by their moral values and in another by what they took to be the imperatives of the law they were asked to enforce. An instrumentalist judge simply could not find himself in a moral-formal dilemma, because such a judge could not see the law as something already given to him. The great instrumentalist judges such as Ruffin knew that they were using the precedents to *construct* the law rather than taking the law as given and applying it to the problem before them. They could avoid any dilemmas by constructing the law to conform to their moral values. Horwitz's analysis of instrumentalism in antebellum law helps us understand even more why Judge Ruffin was not faced with a moral-formal dilemma.

_____

Becoming a Judge: Ruffin's Character

Nothing in Judge Ruffin's jurisprudence fully accounts for the opinion's heightened rhetorical tone, its combination of expressions of regret and firm endorsement of a rule Ruffin describes as harsh. Perhaps the explanation lies in Judge Ruffin's character. Having been only recently appointed to the supreme court, Judge Ruffin was in a position where his performances as judge— the opinions he wrote—would display his character to the public. Or put another way, his opinions were the means by which he constructed his public character. The tone of *State v. Mann* might best be understood as part of that construction. The case's content, its exposition of the logic of slavery, might best be understood as Ruffin's effort to establish, for the entire South, what slavery really required, and thereby to enhance his reputation as a leader in developing Southern law. The rhetoric of *Mann*, its presentation of Ruffin as a person disgusted with the behavior he could not condemn in his judicial capacity, may also have been a way of establishing Ruffin's character as a judge whose interpretation of the law elevated him above the mundane concerns of a person "in his retirement."

Performing civic duties well was one aspect of the Southern culture of honor (as, indeed, was the very idea that men of honor had their civic duties and fulfilled them even at some personal cost). According to Bertram Wyatt-Brown, the South "used the law to combine intellectuality and social utility in a conservative setting." Wyatt-Brown does not focus on judging or even on the law as a means of being an honorable person, and much of his analysis of the law is aimed at showing how deviations from strict legality occurred in the service of the honor culture. Even so, we might profitably examine Judge Ruffin as an exemplar of Southern honor and ask whether his opinion in *State v. Mann* might have been part of his attempt to construct an honorable character in his capacity as a judge.

Judge Ruffin retired from the bench as an honored public servant. On receiving his letter of resignation, a longtime acquaintance who was a member of the state senate said, "To eminent abilities in the discharge of his official duties he has united the utmost uprightness, independence, and urbanity, and no man has left the bench with a more spotless, pure and unimpeachable character." The acquaintance went on to say that Ruffin had infused "into the decisions of the Supreme Court a high tone and moral feeling and sentiment producing the most beneficial results." Another senator referred to Ruffin's "Christian character, and his industry, care, and skill."

In his earlier years, though, Ruffin appears to have had rougher edges. Wyatt-Brown points out that the honor culture is necessarily a hierarchy, and insults coming from some sources might carry no weight. So, for example, Ruffin responded to someone who urged him to respond to a newspaper attack, "No! No!!—The attack is undeserved and not worth answering, come from whom it may: News-papers *cannot* slander a man of the least character." When challenges came from more respectable places, Ruffin took offense. Once he insisted that it was "essential to

[his] reputation" that another lawyer withdraw a remark that Ruffin took to "insinuat[e]" that Ruffin had tampered with a legal document; even after the lawyer complied by writing a note that he had not had "the most remote intention" to make such an insinuation, Ruffin could not let go, demanding that the lawyer explain the remark in open court. Ruffin sporadically received and wrote letters indicating that people, usually other lawyers, cast aspersions on Ruffin's character, although perhaps not more often than any other prominent figure's was questioned.

One judge wrote, apparently years after Ruffin's elevation to the bench, that as a lawyer Ruffin had a "rough and often offensive" manner with opposing parties and witnesses, "hardly ever courteous and not always respectful and frequently abusive." This made him "unpopular with the common people and with many who were not very common." Even as a judge, Ruffin "did not seem to possess that outflowing love of human kind" his mentor at the bar had, and some thought him "overbearing." To create an honorable and respected character, Ruffin would have to turn these characteristics to his advantage.

Judge Ruffin faced another problem, the solution to which also posed an obstacle to developing an honorable public character. For a long time he experienced financial difficulties. He received ten slaves as wedding gifts, and eventually he owned substantial amounts of land. But he regularly confronted financial difficulties. A flurry of letters in December 1818 dealing with legislation affecting judicial salaries suggests that Ruffin's first resignation from the bench late that month was provoked by concern about his low salary. (A few years later a correspondent referred to Ruffin's complaint that the legislature "has Legislated you out of two Courts," but it is not clear what the second of these "courts" might have been—perhaps Ruffin had been using a metaphor about the practice of law rather than offering a description of his judicial service.) In the 1830s, Ruffin's wife hoped that he would move to their plantation and relieve her of the duties associated with running the plantation, but Ruffin told his daughter, "I cannot give up the income arising from my personal exertions." Ruffin may have connected his financial condition to questions of honor. To his eldest son in 1826 Ruffin stressed the importance of keeping careful accounts, undoubtedly a result of Ruffin's own experience. But, significantly, Ruffin added that doing so made it "easy" for him "to shew all my dealings through life and how every dollar that came into my hands has been disposed of"—that is, to demonstrate to anyone who inquired that he was an honorable man.

Hadden emphasizes that Ruffin addressed his financial problems by trading in slaves for five years in the 1820s, a period when obtaining a substantial regular income from his plantations was "doubtful." Ruffin invested four thousand dollars in the initial purchase of slaves, and eventually he made a profit of about six thousand dollars in the slave-trading venture, which ended when Ruffin's partner died in 1826. Although Ruffin was not formally a trader in slaves when he became a supreme court judge, he had been one quite recently. In the 1820s slave trading was not an entirely respectable occupation among honorable men of the South; especially in light of the fact that Ruffin may not have been widely loved as a lawyer, some public performance of honor might have been needed to support his reputation as an honorable man.

Ruffin believed that his public service was a civic duty. Writing in 1813, his longtime friend William Garnett surely expressed Ruffin's own sentiments about Ruffin's legislative service, writing that "the political ocean . . . is a very tempestuous one, . . . but it is necessary that some should buffet the storm, and patriotism requires that no man should hang back when his services are required." When the state legislature threatened to reduce judicial salaries as part of a general effort to make the courts more democratic, Judge Ruffin responded with his own threat of resignation: "I do not covet office for its pay, and can live on my own means and labor," and he would do so if the legislature "destroy[ed] the impartial administration of justice."

The demands of civic duty could be satisfied in several ways, though. In 1828 Ruffin was still a judge on the state trial court when he was offered the presidency of the state bank. He seems to have considered that offer in light of his prospects for becoming a judge on the state supreme court, indicating that the latter position was better because of its pay, permanency, and honor. A correspondent urging him to accept the position as head of the state bank replied, "Honor or Distinction—I neither see nor feel it. . . . I can tell the names of eminent lawyers in many of the States; but the names of judges of the Supreme Court in hardly any one." The legislature was likely to tinker with judicial pay until the reductions "amount to actual or virtual annihilation," and as president of the state bank Ruffin could practice law and earn "more than the salary" of a supreme court judge. Honor, that is, had to be considered as part of a package that included pay, something to which Ruffin might have been particularly sensitive because of his straitened financial circumstances in the prior decade. Ruffin did agree to become president of the state bank, despite receiving the advice that resigning from the bench would prejudice his chances to be appointed to the supreme court. That advice proved erroneous; Ruffin served for only a year as the head of the bank before he was appointed to the supreme court.

Huebner has analyzed several criminal cases Judge Ruffin wrote implicating questions of honor. In contemporary terms, Ruffin was a law-and-order judge who routinely upheld convictions. This of course makes his position in *State v. Mann* even more dramatic, but it weakens the inferences we can draw from specific criminal law opinions upholding convictions, because the outcomes may have been produced by Ruffin's law-and-order inclinations more than by his reaction to the questions of honor the cases presented. Still, some inferences, though weak, are possible.

State v. Crawford (1830) involved a fight between Neil Crawford and Duncan Monroe. During the fight, Crawford bit off Monroe's ear. As Kenneth Greenberg has shown, opposition to physical maiming was an important component of antebellum ideas about honor. Crawford was convicted under a statute prohibiting maiming "on purpose," with the jury instructed that it could convict if it found that Crawford had voluntarily bitten Monroe. On appeal, Crawford argued that the statute should be interpreted to require a more deliberate intent to maim. Judge

Ruffin disagreed, observing that maiming rarely was the entire point of an assault. Rather, it occurred during fights that already had broken out. The legislature could not have intended to make it a crime to maim only when someone deliberately set out to maim. Mentioning "the enormity of the act itself," Ruffin also held that "everything is to be taken against a man who voluntarily maims another."

An extramarital affair gave rise to a murder prosecution in *State v. Craton* (1845). Thomas Harrison, his wife, and his wife's lover left the courthouse where the Harrisons had begun divorce proceedings. Harrison objected to his wife's plan to ride home with Craton, but agreed to allow her to ride with Craton and some relatives. Harrison came across his wife and Craton riding alone and threatened Craton with a knife, stopping his horse in front of Craton. Craton dismounted, picked up a large tree limb, and hit Harrison on the head, killing him. The question on appeal was whether Craton had been provoked, which would have reduced the severity of the crime. Judge Ruffin thought not. Harrison's attempt to stop Craton was "only a lawful impediment to his carrying away the deceased's wife, to her ruin and the husband's dishonor." Harrison's threats were only threats, insufficient to justify the serious assault Craton committed.

Neither of these cases was precisely about honor alone, but in both Judge Ruffin responded to violations of honor. In both cases he refused to mitigate the liability of a person who had behaved dishonorably. To that extent he participated in the enforcement of the Southern system of honor.

Ruffin owned two plantations and a substantial number of slaves (thirty-two in 1830), but he was not active in their management, leaving the plantations to be run by overseers under his wife's general supervision. Like other overseers, Ruffin's were sometimes brutal. In 1824 Ruffin's mentor Murphey wrote him of "the evil and barbarous Treatment of your Negroes by your overseer," who "worked [the slaves] to death" and punished one in a grotesque "barbecue." Ruffin's wife confirmed these accounts. Six years later, after his son William informed him that an overseer was doing a good job "with the negroes and the business of the farm," Ruffin asked his oldest daughter, Catherine, to make sure that Ruffin's wife was well cared for: "I want to make a crop, it is true; but I am more anxious to have my family well served and the domestic kept in due order."

Sometimes Ruffin did express concern about individual slaves. In 1827 he was told that "old Aunt Eve" had been purchased for him for fifty dollars, more "than her value," because of Ruffin's "wishes to accomidate the old lady for her faithful services." Ruffin relied on his personal servant Jesse for important domestic duties and must have felt some affection for him. Ruffin appears to have been a typical absentee owner, taking occasional interest in the lives of particular slaves but being generally inattentive to their lives.

What of Ruffin's views of slavery before he became a judge? Ruffin was apparently an avid correspondent, but relatively few letters written by him survive. Sometimes letters written *to* him suggest Ruffin's views as his correspondents reply to his comments. The letters reflect a great deal of attention to politics, rather less to personal matters, occasional references to domestic matters such as purchasing seed and meat, and even fewer references to slavery—itself perhaps an indication of the place slavery had in Ruffin's psychological universe. As a young student at Princeton, Ruffin apparently expressed some concern, but could not figure out what to do, about slavery. His father replied, "That they are a great, civil, political, and moral evil no Person will deny, but how to get rid of them, is a question which has imploy'd many much more expansive minds than mine, without fixing on any rational, or probable means to make their situations more comfortable, without endangering the political safety of the State, and perhaps Jeopardising the lives, property, and everything sacred and dear of the Whites." The letter told Ruffin not to blame anyone today, "for as they are impos'd on us, and not with our consent, the thing is unavoidable." If slaves and their owners lived closely together, owners would exercise "less rigidness of treatment," but "[un]happily for us and them, there are too many with us to render a tolerably free intercourse of sentiment possible." Further, "as there is no tye of gratitude or affection on their parts towards their masters, nothing is to be expected from them, but as fear, servile fear operates on them, which produces a sluggishness of action, which must be increased momentarily by a greater degree of fear."

Ruffin received this letter when he was seventeen or eighteen years old. The structure of argument Ruffin's father developed bears an uncanny resemblance to the structure of Ruffin's opinion in *State v. Mann*. Perhaps as a judge Ruffin drew upon what his father had told him many years before. More likely, though, Ruffin's father drew upon some standard tropes in the defense of slavery, which Judge Ruffin reworked in *State v. Mann*.

With this background we can turn finally to *State v. Mann*. Wyatt-Brown observes that Southern judges "usually enjoyed the highest respect" but "had to be keenly aware of their mediating role" among the South's social classes. Wyatt-Brown's example is a judicial tendency to "adjust" sentences of white offenders "in the direction of mercy." But, according to Wyatt-Brown, the reason for these adjustments was that judges "belonged to the community and could not ignore public feeling." In *State v. Mann*, though, public feeling was reflected in the fact of conviction itself. Ruffin may not have known that Mann's jury was drawn from every rank in Chowan County, although Ruffin was familiar with the county and with Edenton, where he had many correspondents. The fact that the community was willing to convict Mann had to count for something, and Ruffin needed to explain carefully why he was overriding its wishes. The explanation came in two parts: the legal rationale for the result, discussed in Chapter 3, and Judge Ruffin's display of a character that would induce assent to what might otherwise be an uncomfortable judgment.

Judge Ruffin sought to discount the community's judgment on John Mann as an aberration, at least to the extent that that judgment was expressed in a criminal conviction. The opinion asserts, "There have been no prosecutions of this sort." Depending on what Ruffin meant by *of this sort*, this assertion may have been inaccurate; as we have seen, at least one person had been prosecuted in Chowan County in the prior decade for abusing his own slaves without killing them, and there may well have been similar prosecutions elsewhere in the state. Yet Ruffin's readers might not have known of such prosecutions; if they knew of them, they might have understood that Judge Ruffin's opinion rested on—and might have been justified by—his *understanding* of what the community thought about masters' abuse of slaves. Still, this might not have been good enough: A skeptical reader, or one attuned to the community sentiment reflected in Mann's conviction, might have mistrusted the judgment of a person who mistakenly believed that prosecuting a hirer or master for assaulting his own slave was inconsistent with "[t]he established habits and uniform practice of the country." The result alone, that is, could not be its own justification.

The discussion near the opinion's conclusion of other methods of controlling master misconduct might be understood as another attempt by Judge Ruffin to diminish the distance his opinion created between the supreme court and the community that convicted Mann. The passage can be taken as explaining to that community that it had other ways of expressing its condemnation of Mann—through, for example, social ostracism and "frowns and deep execrations."

Judge Ruffin did not attempt to avoid responsibility for the *State v. Mann* opinion's implications, however. As we have seen, he framed his opinion carefully. He knew from the start that he had to place the fact of judgment at the outset, deferring a description of the case's facts until he had prepared his readers for an outcome they might initially find surprising. As his drafts proceeded, his personal responsibility emerged. So, for example, the first draft began with the passive and collective formulation: "This is one of those cases which a Court will always regret being brought into judgment." The published opinion, in contrast, becomes active and personal with its very first sentence, "A Judge cannot but lament when such cases as the present are brought into judgment." After an appeal to his readers' appreciation of the circumstances of Southern slavery, Judge Ruffin introduced in the opinion's third sentence the important distinction between "the man" and "the magistrate" (a more elegant way of saying "judge") restated later in the opinion with a reference to "every man in his retirement"—that is, while not performing a public duty. This distinction conforms to the requirements honor placed on those with public duties.

Some aspects of the Southern experience with dueling, as analyzed by legal scholars, suggest why the distinction between the man and the magistrate might have been important. As Wyatt-Brown and others have emphasized, the honorable man was alert to slurs on his reputation, as Ruffin's letters indicate he was. After learning of such a slur, the honorable man had to seek satisfaction, a public repudiation of the attack on honor. If satisfaction was not forthcoming, the honorable man insulted by a social equal often would escalate the exchange by challenging his opponent to a duel. Eventually, though, respectable Southerners became uncomfortable with the violence associated with dueling, which too often, they came to think, almost randomly deprived the community of people who could enhance it. Initially state legislatures outlawed dueling, sometimes after democratic reforms had given common people more influence. That proved insufficient to suppress the practice. What made a difference were laws disqualifying people who engaged in duels from holding public office. These statutes created a conflict *within* the Southern concept of honor: The honorable person sometimes had to engage in duels, but also ought to take part in public life. The decline of the duel suggests that "the magistrate" prevailed over "the man" in this conflict. Similarly, Judge Ruffin insisted on performing his duty as a magistrate even when it conflicted with his reflections as a "man . . . in his retirement."

Judge Ruffin referred not simply to "the magistrate" but to "the duty of the magistrate," and how he performed his duty mattered a great deal. Again, the opinion's first paragraph sets the tone. Judge Ruffin presented himself as upright, for he would not engage in the "criminal" act of "avoid[ing] any responsibility which the laws impose." This duty overcame any "reluctance" to decide the case as the law demanded. The rhetoric here is quite masculine, calling to mind the nearly impassive man who does his duty no matter how hard it might seem.

Judge Ruffin wrote numerous didactic letters to his daughter Catherine, the first of his fourteen children. In one, dated in 1824 shortly before her fourteenth birthday anniversary, he urged her to be candid in what she wrote. "Candor consists in speaking ones mind truly and sincerely—without malice and without flattery." Candor was important, he continued, not merely because it "makes many friends," but more important because "it has a very powerful tendency to make us *better* within ourselves." The candor Ruffin displayed in *State v. Mann* helped him explain—to himself as well as to his readers—how he was a good person notwithstanding the harshness of the law he made and enforced. When in *The Key to Uncle Tom's Cabin* Stowe praised Judge Ruffin's "noble scorn of dissimulation" and referred to his opinion as "dignified," she perhaps ironically confirmed his success in constructing himself as a Southern gentleman of honor.

Ruffin may have taken some pride in the honesty of his opinion. Ruffin regarded his adolescent son William as something of a slacker. Chastising William for concealing a certain profligacy, Ruffin wrote, "If it were always safe, and pleasant to do what is right, who would ever err!" *State v. Mann* was right, and in some ways its correctness was confirmed for Ruffin by the opinion's open acknowledgement that it was not safe or pleasant to write.

A less important facet of the relation between Judge Ruffin's role in the family and his actions as a judge can be seen in another part of the same letter. Ruffin told his son, "I would not wound, but to cure you; I would not admonish, but to improve you." Here Ruffin expresses the understanding of the domestic relation of parent to child that he wrote into *State v. Mann*. In families, discipline was aimed at improving the child, something Ruffin thought absent from the relation of master and slave in the pure form that he had to accept for legal analysis. Here Ruffin almost expressly disclaims a position popular among Southern defenders of slavery, that slavery was a benevolent, paternalistic relationship between the master as father and the slave as child. Instead Ruffin presents slavery unalloyed by paternalism. Ruffin's realism and political sophistication—and his experience as a father and slaveowner—may have forced the contrast between domestic relations and slavery on him, making it natural for him to distinguish between domestic relations and slavery as he did.

Judge Ruffin's opinion conforms to the demands of honor in a final way. The opinion's deepest assumption is that slaves were human beings, not different in any moral respect from their owners. Ruffin explained that moderate discipline in domestic relations was sufficient because children and apprentices could be offered explanations for apparently onerous requirements that they, as reasonable people, could appreciate as justifying the requirements. No such explanations could be offered to slaves, but not because they were unable to appreciate moral reasoning. Judge Ruffin refused to treat slaves as so "stupid" as to accept "moral considerations" that would explain why the slave should "live without knowledge and without the capacity to make anything his own, and to toil that another may reap the fruits." Precisely because slaves were moral beings, the only method of sustaining slavery was the master's absolute power.

It will not have escaped notice that Lydia has almost disappeared from this account of *State v. Mann*. If solid information about John Mann is hard to discover, I found it impossible to locate information about Lydia. And yet one possibility remains, though historians cannot easily exploit it. I believe that there is a decent chance that some African American family has an oral tradition about life under slavery, including a story about an ancestor who was wounded by her temporary master in just the way described in *State v. Mann*. Someday a member of that family may connect the family's oral tradition to *State v. Mann*—perhaps after reading this account. If that happens, historians will gain a better understanding of the case.

CHAPTER 5

The Novel

Harriet Beecher Stowe, the author of the best-selling antislavery novel *Uncle Tom's Cabin*, made Judge Ruffin's opinion in *State v. Mann* a central feature of her second antislavery novel, *Dred: A Tale of the Great Dismal Swamp*. Contemporary scholars have rediscovered *Uncle Tom's Cabin*, finding in it more literary merit than the past few generations of readers did. *Dred* has been neglected, in part because it is much weaker as a novel than *Uncle Tom's Cabin*. Stowe's second antislavery novel, though, is in some ways more interesting than her first. While not as good in literary terms, *Dred* presents a more complex argument about why the pervasive adoption of Christian values throughout society was the only possible means by which the United States could rid itself of slavery and its evils.

Why Stowe Wrote Her
Second Antislavery Novel

Southern defenders of slavery were outraged by the popular success of *Uncle Tom's Cabin* (1852). They believed that it grossly misrepresented slavery as it existed in the South. William Gilmore Simms, one of the South's leading literary figures, thought it absurd to locate Simon Legree's brutality isolated on a plantation in Louisiana "where his conduct comes under no human cognizance."

The book was controversial in some Northern circles as well. As Stowe's biographer Joan Hedrick puts it, in one chapter Stowe "let loose her fury against the American clergy whose pronouncements . . . supported the abomination of slavery." She quoted one "American divine" as asserting that slavery "had no evils but such as are inseparable from any other relations in social and domestic life." That "divine" was the Reverend Joel Parker, an acquaintance of Stowe's father and husband, themselves both ministers. Parker was offended at the attribution to him of a sentiment that, by equating slavery with other domestic relations, seemed to accept slavery as no worse than marriage and the family. Parker's actual statement had been a bit more qualified, asserting that "the evils inseparable from slavery" were no different from those "equally inseparable from depraved human nature in other lawful relations." This could have been taken as a critique of fallen human nature in all its relations or as a criticism of marriage as well as of slavery, but, as Hedrick notes, it was generally taken to cloak slavery with whatever moral approval already attended marriage and the family.

Parker's cause was taken up by the *Observer*, a proslavery New York newspaper, whose editorial writer criticized *Uncle Tom's Cabin* for its "decidedly anti-ministerial" stance. Stowe responded with a letter to the newspaper's editor in which she said that her initial impulse was to take "refuge in that sanctuary of silence which is the most proper resort of a christian woman when assailed by abuse of any kind." But, as Hedrick observes, "[t]he 'sanctuary of silence' was not congenial" for Stowe.

Writing in the *Observer*, Parker challenged Stowe to show that she had accurately described the views of slavery held by ministers. Stowe responded enthusiastically to the challenge. She told one of her brothers that another was "already up to his chin in documents which he reads & makes notes of." She asked her brothers to locate "a few declarations selected from the back files" of the *Observer* and to contact Lewis Tappan, a prominent businessman who financed Northern antislavery activism, to see "if he has any thing on his shelves." The *Observer* did not publish the results of Stowe's research efforts, but the controversy with Parker, and the Southern reaction to *Uncle Tom's Cabin*, led Stowe into a book-length defense of the novel's factual premises.

Stowe had been pushed into writing *Uncle Tom's Cabin* by her literary ambitions, her deep religious feelings, and the enactment of the Fugitive Slave Law in 1850. Writing the novel, Stowe built upon "observation, incidents which have occurred in the sphere of my personal knowledge, or in the knowledge of my friends," as she put it in a letter proposing that the *National Era*, an antislavery newspaper, publish the novel in serial form. Harriet Beecher had been born and raised in Connecticut, where she received an education pervaded by Calvinist religion. After graduating from a Hartford seminary, Harriet moved with her father and sister to Cincinnati, Ohio, where her father became the first president of the Lane Theological Seminary. Harriet and her sister started a school for young women, and in 1834 Harriet married Calvin Stowe, a widower who taught biblical literature at Lane. The Stowes lived in Cincinnati until 1850, when they moved to Maine, where Calvin Stowe became a professor at Bowdoin College.

Cincinnati, located on the Ohio River and bordering on the slave state of Kentucky, was a major internal port, through which many Southerners passed as they went north and west, often with their slaves. Stowe learned about the South from family acquaintances from the South, including ministers who traveled throughout the region, and from some of the fugitive slaves who escaped through the city. Eliza Buck, the family's cook, was, according to Stowe, "a regular epitome of slave life in herself, fat, gentle, easy, loving and loveable," who told Stowe "the whole sad story of a Virginia-raised slave's life," including stories about being "sold on to a plantation in Louisiana . . . without any warning." Buck told Stowe "of scenes on the Louisiana plantations & how she has often been out in the night by stealth, ministering to poor slaves, who had been mangled & lacerated by the whip."

———

Stowe Discovers Judge Ruffin

As Stowe was preparing *Uncle Tom's Cabin*, she sought to broaden the base of information she could use in it, asking her friends for information, and even as early episodes appeared she continued to solicit information that she might use in later ones. Probably the most important source for factual information Stowe incorporated into *Uncle Tom's Cabin* was Theodore Dwight Weld's *American Slavery As It Is*, which had been published in 1839. Later Stowe told Weld's wife, the abolitionist and feminist leader Angelina Grimké Weld, that she "slept with *American Slavery* under her pillow as she wrote *Uncle Tom's Cabin*."

Nonetheless, Stowe compiled much more factual information *after* the book was published than she had in hand while she was writing it. In 1853 she published *A Key to Uncle Tom's Cabin: Presenting the Original Facts and Documents upon Which the Story Is Founded*. This work, as Hedrick says, "corroborates [Stowe's] portraits after the fact." Stowe wrote a friend, "I must confess, that, until I commenced the examination necessary to write [*A Key*], I had not *begun* to measure the depth of the abyss." Among the materials Stowe consulted, and presented, were legal materials: cases, statutes, and reports of legal proceedings. Weld had relied on similar sources, of course, but Stowe seems to have been particularly struck by her examination, or reexamination, of the legal materials: "The law, records of courts, & judicial proceedings are so incredible, as to fill me with amazement whenever I think of them." *State v. Mann* seems to have made an especially strong impression.

Early in *A Key* Stowe insisted that her aim in *Uncle Tom's Cabin* was "to separate carefully, as far as possible, the system from the men." So, for example, she had created a character, Augustine St. Clare, to exemplify the humane master, an "aristocrat by nature . . . who, though he may be just, generous and humane, to those whom he considers his equals, is entirely insensible to the wants, and sufferings, and common humanity, of those whom he considers the lower orders." Southern critics of *Uncle Tom's Cabin* had been particularly severe on Stowe's description of Simon Legree's murder of Tom. Stowe replied in part by demonstrating that, while the brutal murder of slaves by the owners was nominally unlawful, in fact masters killed their slaves under circumstances that ought to have been called murder. But, perhaps more important, she used Legree to emphasize that slavery as an institution was entirely independent of the characters of slaveowners: "*[N]o Southern law requires any test of* CHARACTER *from the man to whom the absolute power of master is granted.*" Echoing language from *State v. Mann*, Stowe continued, "[T]he legal power of the master amounts to an absolute despotism over body and soul" and asked "whether this awful power to bind and to loose, to open and to shut the kingdom of heaven, ought to be instructed to every man in the community, without any other qualification than that of property to buy."

The question of character recurred in her treatment of Judge Ruffin himself. On the basis only of his opinion in *State v. Mann*, Stowe included Ruffin in the class of "men of honor, men of humanity, men of kindest and gentlest feelings," who were "*obliged* to interpret these severe laws with inflexible severity" because of their fear of the slave population, "that seething, boiling tide, never wholly repressed." Judges might write opinions that diminished the strictures of slavery, if only they would "listen to the voice of their more honorable nature," but according to Stowe, "[s]uch decisions do not commend themselves to the professional admiration of legal gentlemen."

The theme that we should contrast a cool law and logic with warm humanity pervades Stowe's treatment of Southern slave law. She referred to a "cool legal humanity" and described a "cool-blooded course of remark." Some "revolting" decisions were nonetheless "strictly logical and legal." Introducing a long quotation from *State v. Mann*, Stowe wrote that Judge Ruffin's "remarks . . . are so characteristic, and so strongly express the conflict between the feelings of the humane judge and the logical necessity of a strict interpreter of slave-law, that we shall quote largely from it." She continued, "One cannot but admire the unflinching calmness with which a man, evidently possessed of honorable and humane intentions, walks through the most extreme and terrible results and conclusions, in obedience to the laws of legal truth." More generally, "every act of humanity from every individual owner is an illogical result from the legal definition." At least twice Stowe commented more extensively in *A Key* on such acts of humanity within the legal system itself. When judges did respond to cases that were "so loathsome and frightful, that the judge prefers to be illogical, rather than inhuman" by qualifying the logic of slavery as expressed in *State v. Mann*, Stowe called the decisions "generously inconsistent with every principle and precedent of slave jurisprudence, and we bless God for it." In another instance, Stowe began by reiterating her argument that "justice has been turned away backward by the land of law, and equity and common humanity have been kept out by the bolt and bar of logic," but then praised a prosecution "in which the nobler feelings of the human heart have burst over formalized limits" by men "who were not ashamed of possessing in their bosoms that very dangerous and most illogical agitator, the human heart."

Legal historian Alfred Brophy has shown that Stowe's concern about the conflict between the law's logic and the heart's morality pervaded *Uncle Tom's Cabin*. Brophy categorizes Stowe's understanding of slave into several categories: the law's failure to protect slaves, its interference with humane treatment of slaves, and the sanction it gave to "releas[ing] cruel human nature from any outside restraints." These failures meant that honorable people had to look outside the law for guidance, and might even break the law in the service of humanity. Brophy points to an early chapter in *Uncle Tom's Cabin* to illustrate Stowe's willingness to accept action that violated the law in the service of a higher good. Two fugitive slaves arrive at the house owned by a politician who had recently voted to make it a crime to harbor such fugitives. The fugitives' arrival interrupts a "dialogue" between the politician and his wife over the new law. The politician tries to reason with his wife, who responds, "I hate reasoning." In the end, the politician does harbor the fugitives, and takes them to a Quaker settlement where they can live freely. As he prepares to leave, his wife says, "Your heart is better than your head."

The intellectual historian Perry Miller demonstrated that the contrast between the heart and the head was central in antebellum thought about law in America. Law was logical and often inhumane, while the human heart responded to the illogical tugs of sentiment. Stowe's treatment of law in *Uncle Tom's Cabin* and in *A Key* fits nicely into the framework Miller developed. Stowe's criticism in the two books of the ministers who supported slavery suggested social reform could occur only outside institutions like organized religion, through individual moral salvation. *Uncle Tom's Cabin* emphasized the role of Christian belief in liberating slaves, but not the role of any organized institution.

Dred: Stowe's Second
Antislavery Novel

Three years after she published *Uncle Tom's Cabin*, Stowe again took up the question of slavery. In *Dred: A Tale of the Great Dismal Swamp* Stowe gave *State v. Mann* an important place in the plot. Indeed, as one literary scholar puts it, "legal matters are so central to *Dred* that it seems to have been written primarily to give them a context." Dred, a leader of a slave rebellion, plays an important part in the novel, but there is no solid evidence that Stowe named the character having in mind Dred Scott, the subject of the Supreme Court's 1857 decision invalidating the Missouri Compromise (which had limited the territorial expansion of slavery), a decision that helped precipitate the Civil War. In one scholar's words, Stowe "started writing the book before the case began receiving media attention and finished it before the Supreme Court reached its decision." On the other hand, Stowe *was* in the process of writing the novel after the Dred Scott case arrived at the Supreme Court in February 1856 and started to gain attention in the newspapers, and the title character appears first about halfway through the novel. Introducing the character, Stowe wrote that his name was "not unusual among the slaves, and [was] generally given to those of great physical force."

Just as Stowe had written *Uncle Tom's Cabin* with the Compromise of 1850 in the background, so too were national events in the background of *Dred:* the national controversy over whether slavery would be allowed in Kansas and Nebraska, John Brown's armed raid on Pottowatomie in Kansas in May 1856, and the caning of Massachusetts Senator Charles Sumner by Southerner Preston Brooks on the Senate floor in the same month. Stowe wrote *Dred* in about three months in mid-1856.

Hedrick says accurately enough that *Dred* is "not a good novel," containing "insufficiently imagined characters [and] stilted dialogue," and suggests that the speed with which Stowe wrote the novel accounts in part for its weaknesses. Plot coincidences abound, inserted, so it seems, so that Stowe could make her didactic points. Often characters serve primarily as vehicles for viewpoints—rigid types, in another scholar's words—rather than as realized depictions of actual human beings. Thomas Wentworth Higginson observed that "Mrs. Stowe's 'Dred' seems dim and melodramatic beside the actual Nat Turner," the Virginian whose organization of a slave rebellion provoked widespread Southern anxiety. The book is filled with speeches expounding positions that Stowe wishes to criticize or endorse; the excerpts from those speeches in the remainder of this chapter do not misrepresent their overall literary quality.

Yet *Dred* supplies something that *Uncle Tom's Cabin* lacks. Stowe's first novel *asserted* that Christian salvation could rid the nation of slavery; *Dred* presented an argument that nothing else could. Thematically, *Dred* examines law, politics, and rebellion as means of eliminating slavery, and finds all three wanting. As literary historian Lisa Whitney puts it, the success of *Uncle Tom's Cabin* may have enabled Stowe "to explore more complicated and rigorous moral questions in *Dred*," pushing her "to plunge into dilemmas less easily and satisfactorily dealt with." At *Dred*'s conclusion, Christian salvation is all that remains. But the novel's failure as a novel suggests that even Christian salvation may not succeed.

Dred was initially published in serial form, as was *Uncle Tom's Cabin*, but it reflects its origins much more obviously: It is quite episodic and less integrated than Stowe's first antislavery novel. The spine of the plot involves the courtship of Nina Gordon, a young heiress of one North Carolina plantation, by Edward Clayton, the owner of another plantation. Edward's father is the state's chief justice, who eventually renders the opinion in *State v. Mann*, although the decision's legal context differs from *State v.*

Mann itself in interesting ways. Nina Gordon's brother Tom, a politician, also represents slavery's defenders. Harry Gordon, the half-brother of Nina and Tom, is a slave in the household, the son of their father and one of his slaves. Finally, Dred, who actually plays a rather small but structurally important role in the novel that bears his name, is the leader of a group of slaves who live in North Carolina's Great Dismal Swamp and plan a slave rebellion.

We can organize many of *Dred*'s episodes around four candidates for achieving the good society by reforming and eventually eliminating slavery: the law, religion, politics, and rebellion. Stowe associates the law with reason and finds both inadequate to the task of reform. She argues that the politics of amelioration is inconsistent with slavery's deepest commitments as revealed in existing law. She treats rebellion as un-Christian and therefore to be rejected. Finally, she distinguishes between what she calls the "degenerate Christianity of the slave states" and true Christianity, which she associates closely to feminine sentiment and which she finds to be the only real hope for social reform. Not addressing this last possibility, literary scholar Brook Thomas accurately describes *Dred* as "dramatiz[ing] Edward's inability to find alternatives to slavery within the South."

Law in *Dred*

Stowe uses an episode that begins with Tom Gordon's sexual harassment of a slave to illustrate the conflict between law on the one hand and a sentimentalized and feminized religion on the other. Tom addresses Lisette, the slave who is also Harry Gordon's wife, in excessively familiar terms and places his hands on her in a clearly sexualized approach. Harry interrupts the scene, saying that Nina is observing as well. Nina comes to Lisette's defense, and Tom retreats, intimating that he intends to purchase Lisette from her owner. Nina tells Harry that she will buy Lisette herself, but Harry says that Nina does not have the money to do so. Nina replies, "I'll mortgage the plantation, before Tom Gordon shall do this thing!" Nina also promises to set Harry free, through a private bill of manumission to be submitted to the state legislature. Nina then borrows the necessary funds from Edward Clayton and purchases Lisette.

Another, less attractive transaction follows this humanitarian one. Mr. Jekyl, a lawyer, has located property—a Mississippi plantation with its slaves—to which Tom and Nina Gordon are entitled. Jekyl, a pompous sort whose utilitarian philosophy—which Stowe refers to as a theology—plays an important role throughout the book, describes the situation: The Gordons' aunt inherited the plantation from her husband. She died and left it to her son, who, as Mr. Jekyl puts it, "lived in a very reprehensible union with a handsome quadroon girl [whose name, we later learn, is Cora]. . . . [S]he, being an artful creature, I suppose, as a great many of them are, got such an ascendancy over him, that he took her up to Ohio, and married her." Before leaving the state, the son (the Gordons' cousin) filed what Mr. Jekyl calls "a deed of emancipation" in Mississippi. The couple lived in Ohio for several years and had two children there. By moving to Ohio and having the emancipation deed in Mississippi, he believed, she had become a free woman. The husband died and left the plantation to his wife. Cora returned to Mississippi and took possession of the plantation. Mr. Jekyl met a disgruntled overseer there and began looking into the facts. He discovered that "as the law stood, the deed of emancipation was no more than so much waste paper." As a result, "she and her children are just as much slaves as any on her plantation." And the owners were the Gordons: "The act of emancipation was contrary to law, and, though the man meant well, yet it amounted to a robbery of the heirs."

After Mr. Jekyl finishes, Nina asks him to confirm that he is an elder in his church. When Mr. Jekyl does so, Nina says, "I am a wild young girl, and don't profess to know much about religion; but I want you to tell me, as a Christian, if you think it would be *right* to take this woman and children, and her property." For Mr. Jekyl, the answer is obvious: "Why, certainly, my dear Miss Gordon; is n't it right that every one should have his own property." Mr. Jekyl says that he "view[s] things simply with the eye of the law; and, in the eye of the law, that woman and her children are as much your property as the shoe on your foot." Nina hopes, though, "that you might see with the eye of the Gospel, sometimes!" Nina invokes the Golden Rule, asking whether in doing this she would be doing as she should wish to be done by. Mr. Jekyl replies, "My dear Miss Gordon, young ladies of fine feeling, at your time of life, are often confused on this subject by a wrong application of the Scripture language. Suppose I were a robber, and had possession of your property? Of course, I should n't wish to be made to give it up. But would it follow that the golden rule obliged the lawful possessor not to take it from me?" Stowe concludes the exchange with this observation: "Like many other young persons, Nina could *feel* her way out of a sophistry much sooner than she could think it out, and she answered to all this reasoning, 'After all, I can't think it would be right.'"

There is one further point. After Nina leaves the room, Tom urges Mr. Jekyl to go forward immediately: "You see, her pet nigger, this Harry, is this woman's brother; and if she gave him the word, he'd write at once, and put her on the alarm." By linking Harry and the owner of the Mississippi plantation, no matter how clumsily, Stowe raises questions for the reader about whether Nina will be able to carry out her promise to emancipate Harry.

Later Edward learns from Mr. Jekyl that Cora had escaped to Cincinnati from Tom Gordon's plantation. After she was apprehended as a fugitive, she and her children were put up for sale. Edward travels to the site of the sale, only to discover that Cora Gordon is in jail awaiting trial for killing her children to keep them from being returned to slavery. Addressing the court, Cora explains her actions, saying that she was "willing to give up my soul to save theirs." In the course of her statement, Cora also refers to the law as the source of her re-enslavement: "My children were born to liberty; they were brought up to liberty, till my father's son entered a suit for us, and made us *slaves*. Judge and jury helped him—all your laws and your officers helped him—to take away the rights of the widow and the fatherless!"

The episode with Mr. Jekyl is based on an 1838 Mississippi case, *Hinds v. Brazealle*. Stowe places the case in a framework of law, religion, and sentiment. Stowe does not question that the Gordons' legal rights are what Mr. Jekyl says they are. The law, though, does not conform to the requirements of justice. Mr. Jekyl begins by saying that he sees things only "in the eye of the law," but when Nina asks him to see things with "the eye of the Gospel," he also comes to represent the religion of the slaveholding South, bolstering his legal argument with an interpretation of the Golden Rule that Nina is unable to answer. Even so, Nina's intuitive apprehension of what Christianity truly requires, an apprehension that she cannot explain in words, leads her to an understanding of what justice requires in the face of the reasoned arguments about the law and religion presented by Mr. Jekyl.

A pivotal point in Edward Clayton's life occurs over Stowe's version of *State v. Mann*. Before the decision as recounted in the novel he is optimistic about the prospect for reform of slavery through law; afterward he resigns from the bar. *State v. Mann* has its power over Edward not simply because of what it says about slavery, but because it is rendered in the novel by Judge Clayton, Edward's father. Introducing Judge Clayton, Stowe describes him as a "gentleman of the old school," with "something stately in the position of the head and the carriage of the figure, and a punctilious exactness in the whole air and manner, that gave one a slight impression of sternness." His eyes convey "a calm and decided intellect, of a logical severity of thought" and have a "cold beauty." Stowe continues, "One should apprehend much to fear from such a man's reason—little to hope from any outburst of his emotional nature." But "beneath this external coldness," there is "a severely-repressed nature, of the most fiery and passionate vehemence." Judge Clayton is deeply committed to his family and "strictly and impartially just in all the little minutiae of social and domestic life, never hesitating to speak a truth, or acknowledge an error." Judge Clayton's rigorously logical character is expressed in his legal opinions as well.

Judge Clayton and Edward are affectionate with each other, but Edward is more like his mother than his father—again indicating Stowe's linking of reason with the male and sentiment with the female. Judge Clayton is "obliged constantly to point out deficiencies in [Edward's] reasonings, founded more on a keen appreciation of what things ought to be, than on a practical regard to what they are." For Stowe, however, this self-styled realism is mistaken. Nina, again speaking for "common sense" during a conversation about slavery, says that "anybody's common sense would show that a thing which works so poorly for both sides could n't be from God."

The episode culminating in Stowe's version of *State v. Mann* involves the slave Milly, originally introduced into the novel as the "waiting woman" of Nina's aunt. Milly is "a fine specimen of one of those warlike and splendid races, of whom, as they have seldom been reduced to slavery, there are but few and rare specimens among the slaves of the south." She is a formidable figure: "Her habit of standing and of motion was peculiar and majestic," she wore her usual turban "with a regal air," and her character "was worthy of her remarkable external appearance." She had "the intuitive ability to seize at once on the right and best way of doing everything which is to be done," and "was possessed of that high degree of self-respect which led her to be incorruptibly faithful and thorough in all she undertook."

Many of *Dred*'s episodes implicate the tight financial circumstances of Nina and her family, seeking to maintain a respectable slaveowner's way of life under financial pressure, and this one does too. Milly is hired out to Mr. Barker, a neighbor. One morning Nina, looking out and seeing Milly standing among other slaves, is startled to find that Milly's head is "bound up" and her arm in a sling. Milly tells Nina, "Dat ar man shot me; but, praise de Lord, he did n't kill me! I don't owe him no grudge; but I thought it wan't right and fit that I should be treated so; and so I just *put!*" Examining Milly, Nina finds that Milly's arm "had been grazed by a bullet," producing a flesh wound that had become infected. Milly's head has "a number of deep and severe flesh-cuts." After treating the wounds, Nina tells her aunt, "We'll prosecute those people, and make them pay dear for it." The aunt is less enthusiastic, concerned about the cost, the loss of Milly's time while she is recovering, and the loss of the income from hiring Milly out.

After a short rest, Milly returns, and Nina concludes that "no material injury had been sustained, and that in a few days she would be quite recovered." Nina asks Milly what happened, and Milly tells the story. Mr. Barker "was a mighty nice man," but he had "*two* men" in him, and the other came out when he got drunk. One day Mr. Barker became enraged when he discovered that a slave youngster playing with a burnt stick had gotten one of his recently cleaned shirts dirty. "He swore he 'd kill de chile," who hid behind Milly. Milly "just kep him off on it," and then "he turned on" Milly, using a cowhide whip to beat her over the head. Milly ran out of the room with the child and got her away. Mr. Barker, though, was like "a tiger, — screeching, and foaming, and beating me!" Mr. Barker grabbed his rifle and shot at Milly. "[D]e ball just struck my arm, and glanced off again." Milly ran from Mr. Barker's house into the bush, then found "some free colored folks" with whom she stayed for a couple of days before returning to Nina's home.

Nina again says that she will prosecute Mr. Barker. Milly objects, saying that his wife "is a mighty nice woman, and 'peared like he did n't rightly know what he was 'bout." Nina insists, though, because prosecuting Mr. Barker "may make him more careful with other people." Nina writes Edward Clayton, who returns to her plantation to help. Edward "entered upon the case with great confidence and enthusiasm"—and some pomposity, unremarked on by Stowe. As one of Clayton's acquaintances says, "Clayton has mounted his war-horse." Clayton orates:

> It is a debt which we owe . . . to the character of our state, and to the purity of our institutions, to prove the efficiency of the law in behalf of that class of our population whose helplessness places them more particularly under our protection. They are to us in the condition of children under age; and any violation of their rights should be more particularly attended to.

The lawsuit is filed after a brief investigation that confirms Milly's account. It is Edward Clayton's first appearance in a courtroom. An observer assesses Clayton's chances with the lawsuit, saying, "[I]t really was quite an outrage; and the woman is a presentable creature. And, then, there's the humane dodge; that can be taken, beside all the chivalry part of defending the helpless, and all that sort of thing." Conceding that this is "a very clear case of terrible abuse" and that "the man is a dolt, and a brute beast, and ought to be shot, and so forth," the observer says that the law is on Mr. Barker's side. But he thinks Edward will win the case because he "is a glorious mystifier," who has the added advantage of having "mystified *himself.*"

Judge Clayton reiterates this analysis. For him, the case is "an unfortunate one," because Edward could not win it "if the case goes according to law." But, Judge Clayton notes, "Edward has a great deal of power of eloquence" and "great power of exciting the feelings, and under the influence of his eloquence the case may go the other way, and humanity triumph at the expense of law."

When the case is heard, Edward is indeed eloquent, according to Stowe. "His personal presence was good, his voice melodious, and his elocution fine." But, more important, there was "a certain elevation and clearness in the moral atmosphere around him, — a gravity and earnestness of conviction, which gave a secret power to all he said." Edward's argument tracks the ones Judge Ruffin rejected in *State v. Mann.* Edward urges that the rules to be applied here should be those derived from other "dependent relations of life," where the superior's power to chastise the inferior is "guided and restrained" by law. For Edward, law is founded on concern for *"[t]he good of the subject,"* and "when chastisement is inflicted without just cause, and in a manner so inconsiderate and brutal as to endanger the safety and well-being of the subject, the great foundation principle of the law is violated." His final argument to the jury invokes the "obligation" imposed by the relation of *"entire dependence."* Slave owners must "strictly guard our own moral purity" or otherwise "degenerate into despots and tyrants." The judge charges the jury to find for the plaintiff if the punishment inflicted on Milly was disproportionate and cruel, and, "with little discussion," the jury unanimously does so.

Eventually the case is appealed to the state supreme court, on which Judge Clayton sits. He is "exceedingly chagrined," because he knows that he will have to reverse the verdict and take away Edward's victory: "What I see, I must speak, though it go against all my feelings and all my sense of right." He accepts his wife's description of reversing the decision as "the most monstrous injustice," but says, as Robert Cover's formalist judge might, "I sit in my seat, not to make laws, nor to alter them, but simply to declare what they are." Before a courtroom in which Edward Clayton, Mr. Barker, and Harry Gordon are seated, Judge Clayton reads the court's decision, which is *State v. Mann* word-for-word.

Edward Clayton listens to the opinion and observes its effect on Harry: "Never had Clayton so forcibly realized the horrors of slavery as when he heard them thus so calmly defined in the presence of one into whose soul the iron had entered. The tones of Judge Clayton's voice, so passionless, clear, and deliberate; the solemn, calm, unflinching earnestness of his words, were more than a thousand passionate appeals." After his father finishes reading the opinion, Edward asks for permission to speak, which the court, "slightly surprised" but curious, grants. Edward says that the decision showed to him, "for the first time," the true nature of the law of slavery and of slavery itself. "I had before flattered myself with the hope that it might be considered a guardian institution, by which a stronger race might assume the care and instruction of the weaker one." But, he continues, "[t]his illusion is destroyed. . . . I cannot, therefore, as a Christian man, remain in the practice of law in a slave state. I therefore relinquish the profession, into which I have just been inducted, and retire forever from the bar of my native state." His father, "with unaltered composure, . . . proceeded to the next business of the court."

Edward returns home, and two days later he talks with his father about Edward's decision—and Judge Clayton's. Judge Clayton begins by asking whether Edward has decided to stop owning slaves. Edward replies that he has done so "so far as my own intentions are concerned," but will continue to own slaves "as a means of protecting my servants from the cruelties of the law." Judge Clayton asks what Edward will do if protecting his slaves brings him into conflict with the law. Edward responds that he will do everything he can to change the law. His father presses him: "[S]uppose the law is so rooted in the nature of the institution, that it cannot be repealed without uprooting the institution?" Edward would repeal the law anyway. Judge Clayton agrees that that is "the logical line of life." But, he says, "communities do not follow such lines." Edward would be "in opposition to the community in which you live." Then, Edward replies, he might have to move elsewhere. Perhaps resigned to that outcome, Judge Clayton says, "Every man must act up to his sense of duty."

Judge Clayton then uses Edward's actions to explain and defend his own. "Human law is, at best, but an approximation, a reflection of many of the ills of our nature. Imperfect as it is, it is, on the whole, a blessing." Edward asks why his father did not become a reformer of the system. For Judge Clayton, though, "no reform is possible, unless we are prepared to give up the institution of slavery." That will not happen "till there is a settled conviction in the community that the institution itself is a moral evil." But, Judge Clayton says, he sees "no tendency of things in that direction." The churches "exhibit a degree of moral apathy on this subject which is to me very surprising." In any event, Judge Clayton says that he is not "gifted with the talents of a reformer." As a lawyer and judge, he hopes that he has done more good than evil. He gives Edward his blessing, with the somber thought that "[i]t is of more consequence that we should do right, than that we should enjoy ourselves."

State v. Mann continues to play a role in *Dred*'s melodrama. Edward and Nina plan to marry, but immediately after Edward's conversation with his father, a cholera epidemic comes to Nina's plantation. Two chapters later, Nina dies. Edward stays at the plantation to wind up her financial affairs, and he realizes that all her slaves will become the property of her brother, the brutal Tom Gordon. "The awful words of his father's decision . . . never seemed so dreadful as now, when he was to see this unlimited authority passed into the hands of one whose passions were his only law."

As this account of *State v. Mann*'s appearance in *Dred* shows, Stowe was no lawyer. The suit she describes seems to be a civil suit brought by the owners of the injured slave, of a sort that

Judge Ruffin explicitly said could be maintained. Milly's wounds are apparently trivial, leading to no substantial loss of her working time. Under prevailing legal standards, Nina and her aunt probably could not have recovered any damages from Mr. Barker anyway. But, of course, Stowe was using *State v. Mann*'s description of the logic of slavery as the vehicle for her criticism of slave law. Legal accuracy was unnecessary for her purposes. What mattered more was the sharp contrast she drew between law and its logic on the one side and sentiment and humanity on the other.

Religion, Rebellion, and Politics in *Dred*

State v. Mann returns to the novel one more time, but before we consider its final appearance we need to disentangle the place of organized religion in Stowe's account of Southern slavery. Edward Clayton's resignation from the bar embodies Stowe's conclusion that the law as an institution could not be an instrument for reforming slavery. Stowe's commitment to her version of Christianity made religion and Christianity an obvious alternative to law as an instrument of reform. *Dred* continued the literary confrontation between organized religion and true Christianity that Stowe had begun in *Uncle Tom's Cabin*. There, for example, she had written that "when she heard, on all hands, from kind, compassionate, and estimable people, in the free states of the North, deliberations and discussions as to what Christian duty could be [with respect to returning fugitive slaves to the South], she could only think, These men and Christians cannot know what slavery is."

Portions of *Dred* express the same concern to expose to true Christians what slavery is and to condemn as unchristian the representatives of organized churches who do not oppose slavery. *Dred* contains three appendices whose content indicates Stowe's primary concerns. The first is an extract from the confessions of Nat Turner. The second is a compilation, drawn from *A Key to Uncle Tom's Cabin*, of cases where slaves had been murdered. This appendix shows how the law is one of the novel's thematic focal points. The third appendix is also taken from *A Key*. It summarizes "church action on slavery" and lists declarations by Southern churches supporting slavery. Stowe carefully identifies the institutional affiliations of the people she quotes, the conferences and committees that issued the statements, to ensure that readers understand that she is accurately representing the stance of the South's organized churches.

A critique of organized religion in the South pervades *Dred*. In his conversation after Edward resigns from the bar, Judge Clayton notes the "apathy" of Southern church leaders. For him, "the training of the community" in the direction of reform must begin with church leaders, but, Judge Clayton says, "I see no symptoms of their undertaking it." In the past, he says, churches did speak against slavery, but "[t]hey have grown every year less and less decided; and now the morality of the thing is openly defended in our pulpits, to my great disgust."

In one interlude Edward Clayton visits his uncle Dr. Cushing, "a popular and much-admired clergyman," who seems to Edward to agree with Edward about "the terrible evils of the slave system." Dr. Cushing, though, is "a peace-maker, a modifier, and harmonizer," and will not take a strong stand against slavery. At Dr. Cushing's house Edward meets several other clergymen. The clergymen discuss the separation of Northern and Southern churches over the issue of slavery. Dr. Cushing attributes the split to "the radical tone of some of your abolition fanatics" and says that he trusts "the softening, meliorating influences of the Gospel" to improve the conditions of slavery. Edward presses him: Has the church ever tried to stop the slave trade, or to prevent family separations? Dr. Cushing concedes that he knows of no such efforts, and he blames "these rabid Northern abolitionists" for making it impossible for the churchmen to make any progress with their moral instruction of slaveowners. The other ministers agree with Dr. Cushing. One calls abolitionists "monomaniacs." Another recounts how he and other Northern ministers tried to stave off the split. Stowe observes that, while this minister believed he was "ready for a millennial charge on the devil," he did not realize that his maneuvering to keep the issue of slavery from dividing the church organization was "not all in accordance with the spirit of the hymn" with which he celebrated his religion. Further discussions lead the ministers to the self-satisfied conclusion that the churches do well leaving Southern slaveowners "perfectly undisturbed, to manage in their own way."

Near the end of the novel, Edward intervenes to stop a beating Tom Gordon is administering to an abolitionist preacher and his family. Edward tells Tom that he should be ashamed of himself; Tom replies by invoking Southern honor and demanding "satisfaction" in a duel. Edward refuses to fight because Tom is not his equal, and the mob disperses, influenced by the "magnetic force" of Edward's "commanding presence." (One of Edward's companions is a magistrate, but, again demonstrating the inefficacy of law, Edward's words and the code of honor, not the magistrate, stop the violence.) In the next chapter Edward meets with Dr. Cushing to try to find a post for the preacher. Dr. Cushing finds the attack on the preacher "shocking" and says that it "shows the necessity of prayer." Edward finds this rather too restrained: "Our house is the state, and our house is on fire by mob law; and, instead of praying the Lord to put it out, you ought to go to work and put it out yourself." Ministers should "make a stand against this" in their preaching. Dr. Cushing says that he would be "glad to do something," but he criticizes the preacher for having been "rather imprudent. . . . We ought to watch against rashness, I think." Dr. Cushing coolly offers to write a letter about the right of free speech, not mentioning any names or even "these particular circumstances." Edward responds that Dr. Cushing reminds him "of a man who proposed commencing an attack on a shark by throwing a sponge at him."

In another conversation between Edward and his father and mother about reform, Edward proposes that the law be changed to allow slaves to receive education, to marry, and to sue for their injuries, to be followed by new laws allowing slaveowners to emancipate their slaves as they choose, keeping the former slaves on as tenants. Judge Clayton is deeply skeptical, referring to the political influence slaveowners have in the legislature: "The holders of slaves are an aristocracy supported by special constitutional privileges. They are united against the spirit of the age by a common interest and danger, and the instinct of self-preservation is infallible." Mrs. Clayton suggests that Edward talk about his proposals with Dr. Cushing, "one of the most influential among the Presbyterians in the whole state" and someone who has "lament[ed] . . . the evils of slavery." But, Judge Clayton replies, Cushing will *talk* against slavery but will not do anything "if the cause is unpopular." The reason is that Cushing "has the interest of Zion on his shoulders, — by which he means the Presbyterian organization, — and he will say that he can't afford to risk his influence. And the same will be true of every leading minister of every denomination." According to Judge Clayton, "None of them dare espouse an unpopular cause, lest the others, taking advantage of it, should go beyond them in public favor." Judge Clayton presents himself as a simple realist, "speak[ing] of things just as they are," and he describes churches as "making practical calculations."

Mr. Jekyl also speaks about religion in practical terms. Cautioning Edward Clayton against excessive enthusiasm for reform, Mr. Jekyl repeatedly invokes practical concerns. Mr. Jekyl, Stowe tells us, "was a theologian, and a man of principle" who was "a point of reference among his Christian brethren." After Edward insists that slaves be "taught to read the Scriptures," Mr. Jekyl urges a practical course. Slave rebellion results when slaves read the Bible, according to him. "The proper way is this: administer such portions only as these creatures are capable of understanding. This admirable system of religious instruction keeps the matter in our own hands, by allowing us to select for them such portions of the word as are best fitted to keep them quiet, dutiful, and obedient." Mr. Jekyl's theology turns out to be utilitarian: True virtue, he believes, "consisted in a love of the greatest good," and "right consisted in creating the greatest amount of happiness." After Stowe describes how Mr. Jekyl's peculiar version of utilitarianism leads him to support slavery, she concludes that his study had made him "wholly inaccessible to any emotion of particular humanity."

Nowhere does organized religion appear in a good light. Nina's aunt, a regular churchgoer who reads the Bible and "preserv[es] a general state of leaden indifference to everybody and everything in the world," reacts to Mr. Barker's assault on Milly with the lament "I shall lose her wages!" Religion offers no solution to the problem of slavery. Stowe evaluates another possibility—rebellion—through the novel's title character, who appears on the scene almost halfway into the book. Rebellion, though, is inextricably religious as well. Harry Gordon has been struck and taunted by Tom Gordon, who alludes to Tom's sexual harassment of Harry's wife. While riding down the road, Harry hears "a deep voice from the swampy thicket." It is Dred, "a tall black man, of magnificent stature and proportions." Dred seems almost like "one of the wild old warrior prophets of the heroic ages," the spokesman for the avenging God of the Old Testament. Dred's eyes burn with an intensity "that betokened habitual excitement to the verge of insanity." Dred speaks in Biblical language, with many references to Bible stories. Dred is also a practical person who "would speak now the language of exaltation, and now that of common life, interchangeably." Excited by Dred's exalted words, Harry vows, "I will not be a slave." Milly intervenes, as she will again, and calms Harry down.

Stowe then devotes a chapter to Dred himself—or, perhaps better, to slave rebellions and their leaders. She quotes from an account of the Denmark Vesey conspiracy in Charleston, South Carolina, in 1822, and then tells us that Dred is one of Vesey's sons, an extremely intelligent young man who at ten was one of his father's confidants. Dred was sold "to a distant plantation," where he was "unsubduable." Dred killed an overseer and fled to the swamps, taking with him only his father's Bible. Inspired by his reading, and isolated from any human contact, Dred sometimes thought of himself as Elijah or John the Baptist. "Wherever he stopped, he formed a sort of retreat, where he received and harbored fugitives."

In a later chapter Dred returns to comfort a fugitive slave who has been mortally wounded by a slave hunter's dog. Dred swears, in Old Testament terms, an oath of vengeance that concludes, "O Lord, avenge us of our adversaries!" Then, appearing at the conclusion of a several-day religious revival meeting, after the revival's leader exhorts the crowd to welcome the Lord, Dred commands his listeners, "Let all the inhabitants of the land tremble! for the day of the Lord cometh!" He continues, "[Y]our hands are defiled with blood, and your fingers are greedy for violence!" Dred's jeremiad generates "a vague, mysterious panic" in the audience because of its implication that violence is coming. Dred slips away, but later he confronts Harry, who chides Dred for his foolishness in putting his life at risk by going to the revival meeting. Dred is unpersuaded: "Harry, did you mark those men? Hunters of men . . . ! Ministers who buy and sell us!" Without directly asking, Dred urges Harry to join a rebellion, but Harry is reluctant because he "won't consent to have blood shed," noting, "My mistress is my sister."

Harry's course toward rebellion really begins when he receives a letter from his sister Cora, who has been re-enslaved by Tom Gordon. As he rides along, Dred again comes out of the woods. Dred presses Harry to "[l]ie in their path and bite them" like a rattlesnake. Finally at least contemplating rebellion, Harry objects that "[w]ithout any means, or combination, or leaders, we should only rush on to our own destruction." After the cholera epidemic sweeps the Clayton plantation and Nina dies, Harry and his wife are slated to become the property of Tom Gordon. Mr. Jekyl returns to take temporary charge of the plantation, and he praises slavery as "a great missionary enterprise for civilizing and christianizing the degraded African." Harry bitterly tells Mr. Jekyl to observe Tom Gordon's management "and you 'll see what sort of a christianizing institution it is." Harry gets increasingly agitated, and when Tom Gordon arrives Harry refuses to kneel on command, saying, "I won't kneel to my younger brother." Tom strikes Harry, who responds with a "violent" blow. Understanding the implications of his action, Harry jumps through the window, runs to his cottage, rounds up his wife, and escapes to the swamp to join up with Dred. Harry soon learns of his sister's killing her children. Dred, reading his Bible, imagines a rebellion "with the calm, immovable firmness of one who felt himself an instrument of doom in a mightier hand." Taking Cora's plight as a sign, Dred tells Harry, "We will go up and take away her battlements, for they are not the Lord's."

Late that evening, Harry and several other fugitives from Tom Gordon and other owners in the area gather in the forest. Dred asks Harry to tell the story of the Declaration of Independence, "while you sit on the graves of men they have murdered!" After recounting the Declaration's list of grievances, Harry asks that "the Lord judge between us and them, if the laws that they put upon us be not worse than any that lay upon them." The Declaration's authors "complained that they could not get justice done to them in the courts. But how stands it with us, who cannot even come into a court to plead?" He tells the group what happened to Milly and recites the court's opinion, which "had burned itself into his memory," "in a clear and solemn voice." One after another, the members of the group rise to tell their own stories. A new member enters the group, and tells Harry that Hark, a slave on Tom Gordon's plantation, is dead, having been scourged all night by Tom Gordon "and two of his drunken associates" who believed that Hark had been communicating with Harry.

Dred then addresses the group: "If they had a right to rise up for their oppressions, shall they condemn us? . . . Woe unto them, for they have cast lots for my people, and given a boy for a harlot, and sold a girl for wine, that they might drink!" He calls on the Lord to awaken: "Wilt thou not avenge thine own elect, that cry unto thee day and night? . . . Wilt thou hold thy peace for all these things, and afflict us very sore?" The group resolves to rise up and smite their oppressors when they receive a sign.

As they conclude, Milly enters. She counsels against rebellion, saying, "If dere must come a day of vengeance, pray not to be in it!" She invokes Christ's torment on the cross: "If de Lord could bear all dat, and love us yet, shan't we? O, brethren, dere's a better way." She says that she's "been in de wilderness" and has "come to Jesus, de Mediator of de new covenant." She has suffered, but when her son was killed, "de Lord turned and looked upon me like he done on Peter." She hated the mistress who had sold her son, but the Lord "judged her poor soul," and she "died with her poor head on my arm. . . . Wan't dat better dan if I'd killed her?" Vengeance should be left to the Lord. "Like he loved us when we was enemies, love yer enemies!" The group is silent after Milly speaks, until Dred rises and tells her, "Woman, thy prayers have prevailed for this time! . . . The hour is not yet come!" Dred's potential rebellion would have been inspired by religion. It is thwarted by religion as well, in the person of Milly. Stowe also addresses the possibility that ordinary politics might help alleviate some of slavery's cruelties. Edward Clayton proposes legal reforms such as the elimination of bans of educating slaves and on slave marriages, but his friend Frank Russel—in some ways the book's most attractive character because of his cynical realism—denies that politicians can accomplish anything. What makes Russel's argument so striking is that he is himself a politician, not averse to reform—or to anything else that might lead to a successful career in politics. After opposing reform, Russel notes, "The noose will change ends, one of these days, and I'll drag the party." But until then he "can't take up that kind of thing. It would be just setting up a fort from which our enemies could fire at us at their leisure." The reason is simple: "Those among us who have got the power in their hands are determined to keep it. . . . They don't mean to let the *first* step be taken, because they don't mean to lay down their power." Eventually Edward becomes convinced that the only effective reform lies in repudiating the rule in *State v. Mann*, which he sees as underpinning the slaveowners' economic and therefore political power.

What solution, if any, does Stowe propose? *Dred*'s conclusion suggests that she saw none within the South—or even within the United States, where in the North former slaves were always at the risk of re-enslavement under the Fugitive Slave Act. Harry despairs of any escape from slavery, but Dred again uses Old Testament language to hold out hope. After receiving a beating, Edward Clayton is nursed back to health by Harry and Lisette in the slave camp run by Dred, whom Clayton observes closely. Dred goes out to fight Tom Gordon and his slave hunters, and dies from a wound in his breast. After Dred's burial, Edward arranges with Harry for the slaves to escape to the North. Eventually he and his sister Anne establish a settlement in Canada, where they live with their former slaves as tenants. Stowe treats this as an alternative to rebellion: For Edward, "nothing but the removal of some of these minds from the oppressions which were goading them could prevent a development of bloody insurrection."

Stowe holds out another possibility, though: religion truly understood, as against the religion expressed in organized churches. Her clearest account of this possibility comes in a letter from Edward Clayton to Nina Gordon, itself responding to a letter from Nina. Nina's letter describes her visits with one of her slaves, "reading to him in the Testament." The very act of reading "waked a new life in me," Nina writes. "Everything is changed; and it is the beauty of Christ that has changed it." Her aunt, learning about this internal conversion, asks Nina to talk with a minister. But, she writes Edward, "I don't think he understood me very well, and I'm sure I did n't understand him." The minister described "three kinds of faith, and two kinds of love; and he thought it was important to know whether I had got the right kind." The talk "only confused me," Nina tells Edward, "and made me very uncomfortable." But, in the evening, she again read portions of the Bible with her slave, and her faith was renewed. Edward's response is enthusiastic. He says that Nina's "childlike simplicity of nature makes you a better scholar than I in that school where the first step is to forget all our worldly wisdom, and become a little child." Men have to overcome their "habits of worldly reasoning." And, most important for present purposes, Edward tells Nina not to be concerned about what her aunt or the minister said. "*What you feel is faith.* They *define* it, and you *feel* it. And there's all the difference between the definition and the feeling, that there is between the husk and the corn."

Nina has discovered a feminized religion of feeling. It operates in her heart. It develops as she reads the Bible with her slave in his cabin, nowhere near any formal church building. That religion—felt but not defined—may be the alternative Stowe offers.

CHAPTER 6

Scholars and *Dred*

Dred resembles *State v. Mann* in this: Both texts provide an entry-way into larger controversies. *Dred* is particularly useful in an exploration of the place sentiment had in antislavery thought and in the abolitionist movement. After describing and evaluating some views of *Dred* offered by scholars of American literature, this chapter concludes by locating *Dred*'s argument about religion as the sole vehicle for reform in a larger historical discussion of the extent to which antebellum abolitionists were interested in reforming institutions rather than individuals.

Literary Scholars Evaluate *Dred*

Compared to *Uncle Tom's Cabin*, *Dred* has received little attention from literary scholars. Joan Hedrick devotes much of a chapter to Stowe's first great book but only three paragraphs to *Dred*.

Dred is a sentimental novel. That genre was invented in the eighteenth century, and it helped expand the audience for novels to include female readers of the comfortable classes. Sentimental novels typically had domestic settings, as *Dred* does in its attention to the ebbs and flows of relations among members of the Clayton and Gordon families. Indeed, *Dred*'s opening episodes deal with Nina Gordon's suitors and her choice among them, a classic theme in the sentimental novel. Sentimental novels were also novels *about* sentiments, exposing their characters' feelings through their words and actions. For sentimental novelists, feelings were more accurate indicators of truth and justice than were reason and law and were better able to effectuate real social change.

The sentimental novel connects to antislavery thought in recent historical analyses of the movement for slavery's abolition. An older tradition connected abolition, particularly in the English colonies, to economics. The argument, made most prominently by the West Indian scholar Eric Williams, was that slavery flourished when it contributed to the development of capitalism in Britain and became vulnerable as its importance to the British economy waned. This argument was never entirely plausible in connection with slavery in the United States, where slavery remained profitable throughout its existence.

Scholars who examined British economic history closely became skeptical of Williams's argument even there. David Brion Davis and Thomas Haskell developed an alternative account of the rise of antislavery thought, still connecting capitalism to abolitionism but less directly. Capitalism transformed personal service into impersonal labor, making all who worked equivalent to each other. In addition, capitalism rested on contracts that people voluntarily entered and for the performance of which they had personal responsibility. People who made such contracts, Haskell argued, became attuned to responsibility more generally understood—that is, to the general requirements morality imposed both on themselves and, importantly, on everyone else, including slaves and slaveowners. The overall effect was to broaden the universe of moral relevance, expanding it to include people previously excluded, such as slaves and, to some degree, women. The movement for the abolition of slavery gained force as the horizon of sentiment expanded, that is, as more and more people were willing to incorporate African slaves into their affective universes, treating them as people "equally capable of feeling" as anyone else. If so, the British literary scholar Markman Ellis suggests, "we might understand the history of slavery better by reading the sentimental novel." Sentimental novels attempted "to reformulate social attitudes to inequality through the development of a new humanitarian sensibility." (Ellis's work deals primarily with the eighteenth century, but his insights seem applicable to Stowe's novels too.)

As literary scholars have suggested, sentimental novels offered what their authors took to be a distinctively female set of solutions to problems of social life. For example, one scholar asserts that *Uncle Tom's Cabin* offers a "vision . . . wherein the Christianized power of motherhood might serve to counteract patriarchal forms of oppression and thereby bring forth a new society based on the female values of self-sacrificing love and nurturing noncompetitiveness," and presents "mothering women and feminized men in *Dred* [as] the only alternatives to male violence and disorder."

Yet, though *Dred* is unquestionably a sentimental novel, it is hardly representative. Perhaps driven by a desire to create ingenious plot turns, Stowe presents a complex set of interracial relations, in which Harry Gordon is the brother of Tom and Nina Gordon and acts as Nina's guide and mentor. The intrafamily relations intersect quite awkwardly with Stowe's critique of slavery, but the novel makes inescapable Stowe's perception that slavery entails interracial sexual relations and their consequences: Harry Gordon is the product of an interracial sexual encounter; Tom Gordon engages in interracial sexual harassment. Further, as Lisa Whitney suggests, the familial ties among the main characters—slaveowners and slaves—demonstrate the impossibility of "an approach to slavery that accepts the familial ideal."

Richard Boyd identifies the "unresolved debate" in *Dred* as "whether Stowe's protagonists ever manage to escape completely the evils of the system they so vigorously condemn." Ellis sees the "attraction of the theme of slavery to the sentimental novel" in "the asymmetrical power relation essential to slavery." On the surface, that asymmetry implicates differences in physical power. For Boyd, violence "runs throughout" the novel, from the violence of slavery itself to the violence done on the abolitionist preacher to the violence offered by Dred in rebellion. Boyd argues that Stowe's depiction of slavery incorporates a mirror image, in which the victims of violence reciprocate by endorsing violence. So, for example, the fact that Harry and Tom Gordon are half-brothers can be read as suggesting that each complements, and in some ways completes, the other. The two men compete on different terms for Lisette, Harry's wife. Boyd evokes an image familiar in the study of slavery, where, following the analysis of the German philosopher Hegel, slavery is said to depend on the *mutual* recognition of master and slave, with the master dependent on the slave for the acknowledgment of the master's status. Boyd argues that Harry and Tom's competition for Lisette "transform[s] . . . the self into a slave of that Other." Tom's effort to assert himself through physical force—one form of violence—is a failure because it relies on "a deluded, naïve notion of power"; Tom "is just as much under the direction of his rival's desire and a slave to that Other as he is master over those slaves to whom he owns legal title." The conflict between Tom and Harry moves from competition to confrontation, culminating in Tom's assault on Harry and Harry's escape to join Dred in the swamp, at least temporarily.

Boyd sees *Dred* as a sentimental novel because the only solution it offers to avoid "the descent of the South into an ever-escalating mimetic violence" is "the stabilizing influence of the matriarchal figure." Violence begins to break out anew just after Nina dies of cholera, for example. "The search for the good, matriarchal model is the primary strategem in the effort to propound an alternative conception of power that might confront and ultimately replace the raw, 'might makes right' ideology omnipresent within Southern slave society." The major attractive characters in *Dred* substitute "self-sacrificing love for coercive domination of others."

According to Boyd, then, *Dred* "rests much of its hope for an alternative to slavery and male structures of domination on the possibility of . . . the power of a benevolent matriarchal model to inspire in others an imitation that brings order and harmony." And yet, Boyd points out, the person who leads others to imitate her is also asserting authority and power of a sort. Escape from conflict may be impossible if the only means of escape reproduces the source of the conflict. Boyd concludes that "*Dred* fails to offer any pattern of human relations that is free of the coercive force of imitative desire, free of that authoritarian kind of mimeticism shown as fundamental to patriarchal slave-holding society."

Boyd's analysis is insightful, but two concerns should be noted. First, Boyd implicitly distinguishes between a type of mimeticism characteristic of slave society and some other type. Perhaps, however, human relations of any sort contain the kind of authoritarian mimeticism that Boyd locates in *Dred*. Second, and perhaps more important for present purposes, Boyd may not fully take into account Stowe's belief that religion could solve the problem of slavery. Boyd incorporates Stowe's attention to religion in his assertion that "Stowe equates motherhood with the divine." But perhaps for Stowe the power and authority of the divine—and therefore, on Boyd's reading, the power and authority of the mother figures who populate *Dred*—may be different in fundamental ways from the masculine power of physical coercion on which slavery rests.

Boyd ends his article discussing Milly, who, as her intervention to halt the slave rebellion indicates, is the "most perfect Christian witness" in the book. Boyd emphasizes Stowe's description of Milly as "one soul" among the "thousands," suggesting that Milly's resolution "is therefore not readily available to the average individual." At the end of the novel, Milly is living alone in New York City, running an orphanage. Boyd treats this "vocation" as "admirable" and "maternal," but says that "its exemplary value seems again quite limited." Her isolation contrasts with the family settings that Stowe seems to value even more.

For Boyd, "Milly's final banishment seems indicative of a deep pessimism over the possibility of a non-violent end to slavery," and "the fictionalized hope in the power of exemplary mother-figures to stem the drift into 'perfect anarchy and confusion' must be judged as futile." Stowe's novel is certainly pessimistic in the sense that it systematically discards one after another solution to the problem of slavery. Still, Boyd may overestimate Stowe's pessimism by failing to appreciate the way that religion figures in Stowe's universe. As Boyd acknowledges, Milly is a saintly figure, and the role of saints has always been not to provide models that everyone can emulate in precise detail but to hold out hope that, by modeling one's life on that of a saint, one can make the world better.

Lisa Whitney argues along similar lines that *Dred* expresses Stowe's decreasing confidence "that the sentimental attitude offered" in *Uncle Tom's Cabin* "would help bring an end to the crisis threatening the peace of the nation." Considering the role of law in the novel, Whitney believes that the "inclusion of this second, competing discourse . . . ultimately dooms *Dred* as a sentimental novel."

On Whitney's reading, the legal discourse and the "sentimental tale of Nina and her domestic world" are "competing explanatory and ordering discourse[s]." For Whitney, "sentimental and legal discourses clash in a way that underscores their mutual exclusivity." The sentimental discourse is feminine; the legal one "belongs . . . almost wholly to men" and "admits no role for female characters and feminine values." Edward Clayton resigns from the bar "because of his own identification with maternal values." Whitney identifies another tension in the novel, between the New Testament values represented by Nina and the domestic scene and Old Testament values. The latter are represented in two forms, by the law and by Dred. As seen in Christian theology, the Old Testament was about law and punishment, and of course Dred "is figured as an Old Testament prophet who castigates society for its betrayal of the law of God." Thus "Stowe sets up a tension in the novel, which is never resolved, between a feminine New Testament vision of meekness, submission, and forgiveness and a masculine Old Testament vision of power, self-assertion, and retribution."

The events in the novel most revealing of the inadequacies of sentiment, for Whitney, occur in connection with Nina's purchase of Harry's wife Lisette to save her from the sexual predation of Tom Gordon, Harry's half-brother. Nina "saves" Lisette by the purchase, but that transforms her from a bystander to an owner; when Nina dies, ownership is transferred to Tom anyway. So "replacing father-rule, based on force, with mother-rule, grounded in sentiment, does not alter the position of slaves." Whitney presses the further point that the purchase, a legal event, reinforces the ties of sentiment that, along with her ownership of him, bind Harry to Nina.

All scholars agree that *Dred* is not an artistic success. The unresolved tensions Whitney identifies are certainly one reason. Yet her own analysis suggests a somewhat different account of the novel. Whitney says that sentiment and law are "alternative interpretive frameworks available to Dred" and his companions. Whitney ties the discourse of law rather tightly to the justification of rebellion. The honesty of Judge Clayton's exposition of the law "frees the slave to act as an independent agent, to fight for his or her own and other slaves' freedom." After he hears the opinion, "the law's passionless definition of slavery ultimately pushes [Harry] toward revolt."

Perhaps it might be better to see Dred as offering a third point to complete a triangle of available discourses, as Whitney suggests almost in passing, writing that the novel "raises the distinctly unsentimental possibility that violent action on the part of African slaves might be required to bring an end to slavery." Yet Dred's rebellion is never brought off, and he is killed not in the course of a rebellion but by a white mob. Dred lives in a swamp but moves easily into the organized community. Literary scholars have pointed out that swamps are "associated with darker, more menacing forces"; swamps sometimes represent the "prospect of a loss of control signified by unlimited growth" and contagion, although Maria Karafilis points out that Stowe is careful to refrain from attributing the cholera epidemic that kills Nina Gordon to the swamp. As Sarah Hartshorne puts it, Stowe "handicapped her hero with a touch of 'insanity' to thwart the very rebellion she was encouraging." Or, in Cynthia Hamilton's words, "slave revolt is not seen as a heroic fight for freedom, but as a spectre of devastation analogous to the nightmare of cholera."

Dred's rebellious impulses may be *based* on Old Testament values of law, but his acts of rebellion do not take the form of legal enforcement of a higher law. The novel's failure may lie not so much in its unresolved tension between law and sentiment as in its unpersuasive rejection of rebellion as a law-based alternative to sentiment. One might see Abraham Lincoln—who reportedly described Stowe on meeting her as "the little woman who wrote the book that started this great war!"—as a political leader who more successfully combined the Old Testament and New Testament values by accepting the necessity for violence to end slavery. As Lincoln put it in his Second Inaugural Address:

> Fondly do we hope—fervently do we pray—that this mighty scourge of war may speedily pass away. Yet, if God wills that it continue until all the wealth piled by the bond-man's two hundred and fifty years of unrequited toil shall be sunk, and until every drop of blood drawn with the lash shall be paid by another drawn with the sword, as it was said three thousand years ago, so still it must be said, "the judgments of the Lord, are true and righteous altogether."

Dred and Abolitionism's "Anti-Institutional" Focus

Writing in 1959, Stanley M. Elkins described abolitionists as "anti-institutional." Stowe's depiction of the failures of law and religion as instruments of reform and her endorsement of individual moral reformation as the vehicle for slavery's abolition appear to fit neatly into Elkins's description of the abolitionist sensibility. Yet there may be more to be said in favor of Stowe's perspective than Elkins thought.

For Elkins, institutions "provide the standards, whereby, for men of sensibility, one part of society may be judged and tested against another." When one removes oneself from thinking about institutions, that person is removed "from the very *idea* of power and how it is used." According to Elkins, anti-institutionalism characterized the segment of American culture in which the abolitionists were located. "Organization was distrusted more or less for its own sake."

Anti-institutional thinkers "exalt[ed] the individual and his limitless potentialities," while expressing their moral views in "high-flown abstraction" that ignored the concrete modes in which moral principles were actually embodied in real social institutions. Without a "daily orientation to institutions," abolitionists could not understand how institutions were "maintained (and, conversely, subverted)." For example, the abolitionists "gave little thought to the use of existing institutions—of the potentialities, say, of the national church organizations." Their reform proposals were, as a result, "erratic, emotional, compulsive, and abstract." Acknowledging abolitionist Theodore Parker's wide knowledge of slavery, Elkins pointed out that even with such knowledge Parker never gave "serious thought to specific improvements in the slave's condition by concentrating on specific features of the institution of American slavery." For abolitionists, "slavery became not really a social problem but a moral abstraction." Their ideas could not "fall into the hands of institutions which could process [them] into concrete proposals." Elkins suggests that abolitionists who thought in institutional terms might have proposed "a series of separate short-term reforms," such as insisting that slaves be allowed to receive Christian instruction and attempting to preserve slave families. Reformers might have promoted policies that allowed slaves to accumulate the funds needed to purchase their freedom.

Elkins's argument attracted some attention from other historians, although less than was given to other parts of his book. Aileen Kraditor criticized Elkins for ignoring divisions among abolitionists. Some, she agreed, were anti-institutional in Elkins's sense. Others, though, did not "repudiat[e] institutions" but "wished to purify them." As Kraditor puts it, "where existing institutions seemed too corrupted they tried to replace them with new institutions through which collective efforts could be exerted."

Stowe was one of the abolitionists of the sort Kraditor describes. Stowe did not ignore the institutions whereby reform might be achieved. Just before referring to "the degenerate Christianity of the slave states," Stowe wrote, "It was far easier to join in a temporary whirlwind of excitement, than to take into consideration troublesome, difficult, and expensive reforms." Stowe *was* discouraged about the prospects for reform, but largely because she believed that slaveowners would not yield their power, not—at least not in *Dred*—because she despaired of institutions in principle. As Brook Thomas puts it in his discussion of *A Key to Uncle Tom's Cabin*, for Stowe "[l]aws should be logical, but they should not support institutions whose logic makes it impossible to exert the influence of sentiment."

Stowe repeatedly contrasts "the practical" with the ideal, to the former's disadvantage. Judge Clayton criticizes Edward for failing to have a "practical regard to what [things] are." Later, Harry recounts to Mr. Jekyl, a defender of slavery, how brutal the conditions on Tom Gordon's plantation are, which leads Mr. Jekyl briefly to appreciate "the difference between the abstract and concrete." Frank Russel, a candidate for the state legislature, engages in a conversation with Edward Clayton about the slave-owners' political domination, and Russel observes, "Why, Clayton, moral sentiment, as you call it, is a humbug! The whole world acquiesces in *what goes*." Here the focus is on the ways in which the particular institutions of power in the slave South depended on slavery and necessarily resisted reform.

Judge Clayton tells his son that a reform program will not work because slavery's defenders "see at once that any change endangers the perpetuity of the system on which their political importance depends." Later Edward Clayton engages in a long conversation with Russel about the prospects for reform. To Edward, legislative reform is the "only safe way of gradual emancipation," and for him the only real reform would be to repudiate the rule of *State v. Mann* and give slaves legal personality. Russel replies that he "can't afford it" because he must "stoop to conquer, at first." Clayton asks Russel "to go with me down to the depths of your soul, where the water is still," where he will see that slavery is "a cancer." Russel readily agrees, but responds that slaveowners "are our masters. . . . Now, if there was any hope of doing any good by this, if there was the least prospect of succeeding, why, I'd join in with you; but there is n't."

Russel asks Clayton to consider supporting a bill against separating slave families—one of Elkins's piecemeal reforms—a practice that, according to Russel, had become so unpopular that "it's rather the fashion to move about that a little." For Clayton, however, passing such a law would be pointless because it would be ineffective unless slaves were allowed to sue and testify, a point

Russel concedes. Russel then returns to the question of power. Clayton again urges reform near the end of the conversation. Slaves "are a patient set, and will bear a great while; and if they only see that anything is being done, it will be an effectual prevention." Insurrection was the alternative to reform. Russel agrees with Clayton that the British aristocracy preserved its power by knowing "when to *yield*," but asserts that the slaveowners of the South intend to extend their empire because "[t]he South understands governing." Clayton concludes the conversation by saying that Russel had omitted "one element of force" from his "calculation": God.

The dinnertime conversation described earlier between Mr. Jekyl and Edward Clayton includes a third character, Tom Gordon. Stowe treats Edward as articulating a sentiment-based antislavery view and Mr. Jekyl as a theologian articulating a sentiment-based proslavery view. Tom Gordon denounces both men as hypocrites. Instead of teaching the Gospel in either the comprehensive way Edward urges or the narrow way offered by Mr. Jekyl, Tom says, "teach them that you 've *got the power!—* teach them the weight of your fist! That's enough for them." Stowe presents Tom as a horrible figure, the Simon Legree of *Dred.* Yet she clearly finds something powerful in Tom's honest insistence that slavery is about power and nothing more than that. In defending his decision to take possession of the plantation he and Nina have inherited, Tom simply says, "Might makes right, — that's my doctrine!" As Whitney puts it, Tom's "virtue is his hatred of hypocrisy." Here too Stowe exhibits an interest in the practical, in the sense of admiring someone who openly describes (and defends) the world as it is.

The role of the practical in *Dred* suggests a different view of Elkins's account of the abolitionists' anti-institutional focus. Elkins writes in passing that at least some abolitionists did form organizations—abolition societies—and participated in churches, especially the Unitarian church with its strongly individualistic theology. Elkins also describes the "showers of antislavery petitions" that Congress received from 1836 to 1844, protesting the "gag rule" that the House of Representatives had adopted, barring any formal consideration of antislavery petitions. As Elkins says, these petitions "were circulated by thousands of volunteer workers," which certainly sounds like a description of some organized activity. Elkins also mentions the "Underground Railroad," which helped slaves escape from the South—again, a form of organized antislavery activity. Focusing on the abolition movement, Elkins said little about the narrower antislavery position of the Republican party and its political predecessors. Kraditor emphasizes these latter organizations, as well as the sustained propaganda campaign against slavery, which was accompanied by "efforts to win elections, pass laws, dominate political parties, reform the churches, and in other ways use institutions to destroy slavery."

Professor of English Gregg Crane uses Stowe's interest in reform through natural justice to argue against the traditional view, developed above, that Stowe uses sentiment "as an antilegal or nonlegal alternative to the law of slavery (as if Stowe were castigating the legal system of slavery from an anarchist position)." To the contrary, Crane argues that Stowe accepted the principles of natural justice that demonstrated slavery's immorality and believed that human institutions could mirror natural justice's requirements. According to Crane, *Dred* expresses the tension between natural rights discourse and positive law "as a conflict between three different theories of legal authority": First, natural rights, "which Stowe expresses in the twin rhetorics of sympathy and revolution"; second, positivism, in which human relations are "governed by power"; and third, "the concept of law as the cultural consensus of the majority." Edward Clayton and, in a different way, Mr. Jekyl are the vehicles for the first view, Tom Gordon for the second, and Judge Clayton in his conversations with Edward for the third.

But, Crane argues, Stowe does not successfully resolve the tensions among the three views in a vision of reformed institutions: "The tension in Stowe's notion of natural rights sentiment between moral emotion as a spiritual form of power and moral emotion as a license for the seizure, possession, and exercise of material power is not resolved." She describes rebellion as a "hopeless project," for example, and does not, in the end, "imagine natural rights fully as the moral consensus and fundamental entitlement of a racially diverse community." "Revolutionary wrath," not law, seems to have more promise, but even it is unavailing because Stowe "fails to envision a black revolution that would reconcile the divided sentiments of sympathy and anger." We can take Crane's argument, in the present context, to be that Stowe's interest in reform through institutions shows the inaccuracy of applying Elkins's characterization to her, but that her failure to develop a vision of law as the means of abolition explains why Elkins may have mistakenly but understandably thought that abolitionists such as Stowe were anti-institutional.

Elkins discounted the abolitionists' activity through organization because the institutions with which he was concerned were "a kind of given," not something that could be developed and used instrumentally. As Elkins saw it, the institutions that mattered for developing concrete policy were those that "provided a frame . . . within which a man pictured himself and the things he might legitimately do with his life." For Elkins, only institutions with a certain fixity, organizations that generated "historic attachments," could provide such a frame. Yet it is unclear why instrumental organizations might not do so as well, albeit a frame that might change as its members' instrumental interests change. Abolitionists were not opposed in principle to institutions through which individuals could structure their lives; they merely opposed the institutions in place that defended slavery. Of course Stowe emphasized the role of God and individual reform, but not entirely because she was anti-institutional. She treated reform as hard work, which unfortunately could not succeed in the face of the slaveowners' institutionalized power. Clayton was willing to work within institutions; it was the institutions that were recalcitrant.

Two features of the intellectual terrain in the late 1950s should be emphasized to help us understand Elkins's perspective and alternative views. First, liberal intellectuals interpreted the McCarthyite movement as the vehicle for marginalized social groups that were anti-institutional in a way that resembled the abolitionists as Elkins described them. This perhaps accounts for the disparaging tone of Elkins's discussion of the abolitionists. Second, and more important for present purposes, *interest-group pluralism* provided the dominant account of how government worked. According to that account, interest groups organized to pursue their self-defined interests. They attempted to elect representatives responsive to their concerns. Something that could be called the public interest resulted from the competition among interest groups as expressed in the legislature.

Influenced by interest-group pluralism, Elkins seems to have assumed that a group was anti-institutional unless it oriented its activity toward legislative influence in the way that modern interest groups did. Recent scholarship developed after reflection on what sociologists call the new social movements provides a different account of the relationship between institutions and government. The new social movements are sometimes described as aspects of *civil society*, which is taken to be something separate from the government. Among the new social movements are feminist organizations, environmental groups, and, importantly, the various groups that helped undermine the Communist regimes in central and eastern Europe in the 1980s.

Theorists of civil society see the organizations of civil society as providing *alternative* "frames" to those offered by the formal organizations associated with the state—or with traditional interest groups. Civil society has its institutions, but they operate outside the state, and are, in Elkins's sense, anti-institutional. They influence government policy nonetheless, not by directly attempting to shape public policy, but by providing alternative locations to the official ones, locations where people can develop their own views about how the good society should operate. In getting together with others, working on common projects, and the like, participants in civil society's institutions develop their own interpretations of social reality, sometimes at odds with the ones supported by official organs of the government. Though they may not directly orient their activity to affecting public policy, civil society's institutions nonetheless may affect that policy by showing officials that there are indeed other courses of action that might be pursued or, perhaps more important, by being ready to step into positions of power when the official order collapses from internal or external pressure, as in the case of the collapse of the Soviet empire and the Civil War respectively.

Dred does not deal with civil society's institutions, and Elkins's description of abolitionists as anti-institutional certainly captures an important element of Stowe's critique of existing institutions. Stowe's emphasis on the role of character and moral reform in producing social reform is similarly compatible with Elkins's account of the abolitionists. Yet Stowe's characterization of the work of reform suggests that Elkins's account should be supplemented by a civil-society one, which helps make sense of the organizational activity associated with abolitionism.

Seeing Stowe and the abolitionists as dedicated to civil society allows us to draw an intriguing parallel to Judge Ruffin's account of slave society in *State v. Mann*. Chapter 3 interpreted Ruffin's opinion as concerned in large part with allocating responsibility for slaveowners' good conduct to the community rather than to law—that is, to the slave society's institutions of civil society. We can see both Judge Ruffin, a defender of slavery, and the abolitionists as committed to the proposition that society is best ordered when the institutions of civil society play a large role, larger perhaps than the role of government's formal institutions. Perhaps, too, we can see them both as anti-institutional in a slightly different sense from Elkins's. Perhaps Elkins should be read as taking the institutions of a market-oriented, bourgeois society as normative, and abolitionists and slavery's defenders as marginalized in such a society—although, of course, on entirely separate margins.

BIBLIOGRAPHICAL ESSAY

Note from the Series Editors: The following bibliographical essay contains the major primary and secondary sources the author consulted for this volume. We have asked all authors in the series to omit formal citations in order to make our volumes more readable, inexpensive, and appealing for students and general readers. In adopting this format, Landmark Law Cases and American Society follows the precedent of a number of highly regarded and widely consulted series.

Thomas D. Morris, *Southern Slavery and the Law, 1619–1860* (Chapel Hill: University of North Carolina Press, 1996), provides a comprehensive study of the law of slavery, summarizing and astutely criticizing earlier works. It discusses the North Carolina cases described in Chapter 1, *State v. Jarrott*, 23 N.C. (1 Ired.) 76 (1840), and *State v. Caesar*, 31 N.C. (9 Ired.) 391 (1849). The Somerset case is discussed in William Wiecek, "*Somerset*: Lord Mansfield and the Legitimacy of Slavery in the Anglo-American World," *University of Chicago Law Review* 42 (Fall 1974): 86–146. Robert J. Steinfeld, *The Invention of Free Labor: The Employment Relation in English and American Law and Culture, 1350–1870* (Chapel Hill: University of North Carolina Press, 1991), contains a discussion of villeinage and its relation to other forms of coerced labor. The most important works on antebellum legal thought, particularly in connection with judicial and legislative regulation of the economy, are Morton J. Horwitz, *The Transformation of American Law, 1780–1860* (Cambridge: Harvard University Press, 1977), and William J. Novak, *The People's Welfare: Law and Regulation in Nineteenth Century America* (Chapel Hill: University of North Carolina Press, 1966), although Novak devotes more attention to the period after 1865 than to the earlier period, and neither book examines Southern law in much detail. For a discussion of moralism in the study of the law of slavery, see Mark Tushnet, "Constructing Paternalist Hegemony: Gross, Johnson, and Hadden on Slaves and Masters," *Law & Social Inquiry* 27 (Winter 2002): 169.

The two cases discussed in Chapter 2 are *State v. Mann*, 2 Devereux (13 N.C.) 263 (1830), and *State v. Hoover*, 20 N.C. 501 (1839). The drafts of the opinion in *State v. Mann* can be found in the fourth volume of J. G. de Roulhac Hamilton, ed., *The Papers of Thomas Ruffin* (Raleigh: Edwards and Broughton Printing Co., 1918–20). An earlier version of the analysis of *State v. Mann* presented here can be found in Mark Tushnet, *The American Law of Slavery, 1810–1860* (Princeton: Princeton University Press, 1981), which also discusses *State v. Jarrott* and *State v. Caesar* in more detail than does Chapter 1. The analysis of *State v. Mann* is critiqued, at least indirectly, in Sally Hadden, "Judging Slavery: Thomas Ruffin and *State v. Mann*," in *Local Matters: Race, Crime, and Justice in the Nineteenth-Century South*, Christopher Waldrep and Donald G. Nieman, eds. (Athens: University of Georgia Press, 2001). This article offers a wide-ranging account of the political background against which *State v. Mann* was decided and an analysis of Judge Ruffin's character as well, and I draw on it extensively in Chapter 4. Sally E. Hadden, *Slave Patrols: Law and Violence in Virginia and the Carolinas* (Cambridge: Harvard University Press, 2001), analyzes another mode of controlling slaves through force authorized by law.

Eugene D. Genovese, *Roll, Jordan, Roll: The World the Slaves Made* (New York: Pantheon Books, 1974), remains the classic modern analysis of slavery, and it includes his important discussion of the ideological and hegemonic function of law, which is also discussed in Tushnet, *The American Law of Slavery*. An earlier work, Eugene Genovese, *The World the Slaveholders Made* (New York: Pantheon, 1969), contains an analysis of the thought of George Fitzhugh that informs both Genovese's analysis and mine. Orlando Patterson, *Slavery and Social Death: A Comparative Study* (Cambridge: Harvard University Press, 1982), complements Genovese's study by developing a model of slavery from worldwide experience.

Abolitionists used examples from the law of slavery to support their attacks on slavery, and both the information their works provide and (perhaps surprisingly) their substantive analysis of the relation between the law of slavery and slavery itself continue to illuminate. Relevant works include Harriet Beecher Stowe, *A Key to Uncle Tom's Cabin; Presenting the Original Facts and Documents upon which the Story Is Founded* (1853; reissued Port Washington, NY: Kennikat Press, 1968); William Goodell, *The American Slave Code in Theory and Practice* (1853; reissued New York: Negro Universities Press, 1968); and Theodore Dwight Weld, *American Slavery As It Is: Testimony of a Thousand Witnesses* (1839; reissued New York: Arno Press, 1969). These works are also available from a number of websites, including *http://www.iath.virginia.edu/utc/uncletom/key/kyhp.html* (for Stowe), *http://www.hti.umich.edu/cgi/t/text-idx?type=simple,c=moa;cc=moa;sld=dbase7987ds23c1f253491* (for Goodell), and *http://www.iath.virginia.edu/utc/abolitn/amslavhp.html* (for Weld) (all visited April 8, 2003).

Robert W. Fogel and Stanley L. Engerman, *Time on the Cross: The Economics of American Negro Slavery* (Boston: Little, Brown, 1974), provides the basic economic analysis of slavery as an institution. Among the works critical of Fogel and Engerman, Herbert G. Gutman, *Slavery and the Numbers Game: A Critique of Time on the Cross* (Champaign: University of Illinois Press, 1975), is probably the most accessible. Jenny Bourne Wahl, *The Bondsman's Burden: An Economic Analysis of the Common Law of Southern Slavery* (New York: Cambridge University Press, 1998), provides an economic analysis of the *law* of slavery, drawing on modern work on the economic analysis of law generally. The most widely used text on economic analysis of law is Richard A. Posner, *Economic Analysis of Law*, 5th ed. (New York: Aspen Law and Business, 1999).

The role of sentiment in slavery and in the law of slavery is a large topic. In addition to Tushnet, *The American Law of Slavery*, Douglas Ambrose, "Sowing Sentiment: Shaping the Southern Presbyterian Household, 1750–1800," *Georgetown Law Journal* 90, no. 1 (Nov. 2001): 143–60, discusses the relation between sentiment and other institutions (primarily religion) as a mechanism of regulating masters' behavior. Douglas Ambrose, "Statism in the Old South: A Reconsideration," in *Slavery, Secession, and Southern History*, Robert Louis Paquette and Louis A. Ferleger, eds. (Charlottesville: University Press of Virginia, 2000), develops the argument in connection with later defenses of slavery. General studies of religion in the South that deal with slavery include Donald G. Mathews, *Slavery and Methodism: A Chapter in American Morality, 1780–1845* (Princeton: Princeton University Press, 1965); Anne C. Loveland, *Southern Evangelicals and the Social Order, 1800–1860* (Baton Rouge: Louisiana State University Press, 1980); and (less extensively) Christine Leigh Heyrman, *Southern Cross: The Beginnings of the Bible Belt* (New York: Alfred A. Knopf, 1997).

Robert M. Cover, *Justice Accused: Antislavery and the Legal Process* (New Haven: Yale University Press, 1975), has been more influential in the literature on antislavery judges than in the literature on the law of slavery, but his identification of a tension between a judge's moral views and the judge's formal position or jurisprudence can profitably be brought to bear on a wide range of problems, as shown by its influence in discussions of modern judges opposed to the regimes within which they work.

Bertram Wyatt-Brown, *Southern Honor: Ethics and Behavior in the Old South* (New York: Oxford University Press, 1982), remains the classic discussion of the Southern culture of honor. It can be supplemented by his more recent collection of essays, Bertram Wyatt-Brown, *The Shaping of Southern Culture: Honor, Grace, and War, 1760s–1890s* (Chapel Hill: University of North Carolina Press, 2001), and Kenneth S. Greenberg, *Honor and Slavery: Lies, Duels, Noses, Masks, Dressing As a Woman, Gifts, Strangers, Humanitarianism, Death, Slave Rebellions, the Proslavery Argument, Baseball, Hunting, and Gambling in the Old South* (Princeton: Princeton University Press, 1996). In different ways, Ariela J. Gross, *Double Character: Slavery and Mastery in the Antebellum Southern Courtroom* (Princeton: Princeton University Press, 2000), and Walter Johnson, *Soul by Soul: Life Inside the Antebellum Slave Market* (Cambridge: Harvard University Press, 1999), show how interactions between slaves and slaveowners constructed the masters' culture of honor, and much more.

The limited information available on the participants in *State v. Mann* is drawn from the 1820 and 1830 census reports. The

"Methodological Notes" in Bill Cecil-Fronsman, *Common Whites: Class and Culture in Antebellum North Carolina* (Lexington: University Press of Kentucky, 1992), suggest why the information from those reports is so limited. Harriet A. Jacobs, *Incidents in the Life of a Slave Girl, Written By Herself,* L. Maria Child, ed., edited with an introduction by Jean Fagan Yellin (Cambridge: Harvard University Press, 1987), provides an account of slave abuse in Chowan County in the late 1820s. It is also available on several websites, including *http://xroads.virginia.edu/~HYPER/JACOBS/hjhome.htm,* and *http://digilib.nypl. org/dynaweb/digs/wwm97255/* (visited April 8, 2003). Christina Accomando, "'The laws were laid down to me anew': Harriet Jacobs and the Reframing of Legal Fictions," *African American Review* 32 (Summer 1998): 229–45, compares Jacobs's account of slavery with the law of slavery. Keith C. Barton, "'Good Cooks and Washers': Slave Hiring, Domestic Labor, and the Market in Bourbon County, Kentucky," *Journal of American History* 84 (Sept. 1997) : 436–60, relies on records kept by an owner of a large number of slaves to examine how slave *hirers* used slaves.

The local history of Chowan County can be found in Thomas C. Parramore, *Cradle of the Colony: The History of Chowan County and Edenton, North Carolina* (Edenton, NC: Edenton Chamber of Commerce, 1967), which relies in part on J. H. Garrett, "A Historic Sketch of the County of Chowan," *Albemarle Times,* May and June 1877. Guion Griffis Johnson, *Ante-Bellum North Carolina: A Social History* (Chapel Hill: University of North Carolina Press, 1937), is a broader history of North Carolina during the period of *State v. Mann.*

Although I do not draw on it directly, Douglas Ambrose, *Henry Hughes and Proslavery Thought in the Old South* (Baton Rouge: Louisiana State University Press, 1996), deeply influenced my thinking about public performances as indications of character. Roscoe Pound, *The Formative Era of American Law* (Boston: Little, Brown, 1938), lists Ruffin as one of the ten finest common law judges in U.S. history. The cases by Judge Ruffin analyzed in my discussion of Roscoe Pound's praise for Ruffin are *Raleigh and Gaston Railroad v. Davis,* 19 N.C. 451 (1837), and

Wiswall v. Brinson, 32 N.C. 554 (1850). James W. Ely, Jr., *Railroads and American Law* (Lawrence: University Press of Kansas, 2001), briefly discusses and evaluates the significance of the *Davis* case. Timothy S. Huebner, *The Southern Judicial Tradition: State Judges and Sectional Distinctiveness, 1790–1890* (Athens: University of Georgia Press, 1999), includes a chapter presenting Judge Ruffin as an example of the tradition Huebner describes. The cases Huebner discusses, on whose treatment I rely, are *State v. Crawford*, 13 N.C. 425 (1830), and *State v. Craton*, 28 N.C. 165 (1845).

Harriet Beecher Stowe, *Dred: A Tale of the Great Dismal Swamp* (Boston: Phillips, Sampson, 1856; reprinted Grosse Point, MI: Scholarly Press, 1968), is also available on line at *http://docsouth.unc.edu/nc/stowe/menu.html* (visited February 13, 2003). Details of the book's creation, and much more, are provided in the prize-winning biography, Joan D. Hedrick, *Harriet Beecher Stowe: A Life* (New York: Oxford University Press, 1994). Additional background information can be found in E. Bruce Kirkham, *The Building of* Uncle Tom's Cabin (Knoxville: University of Tennessee Press, 1977).

The classic exposition of the contrast between law and reason on the one hand and sentiment on the other in antebellum thought is Perry Miller, *The Life of the Mind in America: From the Revolution to the Civil War* (New York: Harcourt, Brace and World, 1965). Alfred L. Brophy, "Humanity, Utility, and Logic in Southern Legal Thought: Harriet Beecher Stowe's Vision in *Dred: A Tale of the Great Dismal Swamp*," *Boston University Law Review* 78 (Oct. 1998): 1113–61, connects *Dred* and *State v. Mann* in much the same way I do. That article draws upon Alfred L. Brophy, "'over and above . . . there broods a portentous shadow, — the shadow of *law*': Harriet Beecher Stowe's Critique of Slave Law in *Uncle Tom's Cabin*," *Journal of Law and Religion* 12, no. 2 (1995–96): 457–506. Brophy also explores *Dred* in "Harriet Beecher Stowe's Interpretation of the 'Slavery of Politics' in *Dred: A Tale of the Great Dismal Swamp*," *Oklahoma City University Law Review* 25 (Spring–Summer 2000): 63–86.

Literary scholars have investigated the rise of the sentimental novel in some detail. Specifically discussing antislavery thought and the sentimental novel is Markman Ellis, *The Politics of Sensibility: Race, Gender, and Commerce in the Sentimental Novel* (New York: Cambridge University Press, 1996). Other relatively general works are Saidiya V. Hartman, *Scenes of Subjection: Terror, Slavery, and Self-Making in Nineteenth Century America* (New York: Oxford University Press, 1997), and Robert S. Levine, *Martin Delany, Frederick Douglas, and the Politics of Representative Identity* (Chapel Hill: University of North Carolina Press, 1997). Articles focusing specifically on *Dred* are Richard Boyd, "Models of Power in Harriet Beecher Stowe's *Dred*," *Studies in American Fiction* 19 (1991): 15–30; Lisa Whitney, "In the Shadow of Uncle Tom's Cabin: Stowe's Vision of Slavery from the Great Dismal Swamp," *New England Quarterly* 66 (Dec. 1993): 552–69; Gregg D. Crane, "Dangerous Sentiments: Sympathy, Rights, and Revolution in Stowe's Antislavery Novels," *Nineteenth Century Literature* 51 (Sept. 1996): 176–204; Maria Karafilis, "Spaces of Democracy in Harriet Beecher Stowe's *Dred*," *Arizona Quarterly* 55 (Autumn 1999): 23–49; Cynthia S. Hamilton, "*Dred:* Intemperate Slavery," *Journal of American Studies* 34 (Aug. 2000): 257–77; Sarah D. Hartshorne, "'Woe Unto You That Desire the Day of the Lord:' Harriet Beecher Stowe and the Corruption of Christianity in *Dred, A Tale of the Great Dismal Swamp*," *Anglican and Episcopal History* 65 (Sept. 1995): 280–99. Crane expands his argument and emphasizes the role of higher law thinking in *Dred* and in U.S. constitutionalism generally in Gregg D. Crane, *Race, Citizenship, and Law in American Literature* (New York: Cambridge University Press, 2002). Brook Thomas, *Cross-Examinations of Law and Literature: Cooper, Hawthorne, Stowe, and Melville* (New York: Cambridge University Press, 1987), deals primarily with *Uncle Tom's Cabin*, but does reflect on the role of law in that novel in ways that illuminate *Dred* as well.

Stanley M. Elkins, *Slavery: A Problem in American Institutional and Intellectual Life*, 3d ed. (Chicago: University of Chicago Press, 1976; 1st ed., 1959), inaugurated the modern era in studies of slavery. Its third part deals with abolitionist thought and has been less influential than its earlier parts. A collection of articles dealing with the book, including one by Aileen Kraditor on the abolitionists, is Ann J. Lane, ed., *The Debate over Slavery: Stanley Elkins and His Critics* (Urbana: University of Illinois Press, 1971). A more recent review of the literature is contained in James L. Huston, "The Experiential Basis of the Northern Antislavery Impulse," *Journal of Southern History* 56 (Nov. 1990): 609–40. There is a large literature on civil society, but the most substantial work is Jean L. Cohen and Andrew Arato, *Civil Society and Political Theory* (Cambridge: MIT Press, 1992).

David Brion Davis, *The Problem of Slavery in the Age of Revolution, 1770–1823* (Ithaca: Cornell University Press, 1975), contributed to the development of the argument that antislavery movements were motivated by ideological concerns, not economic ones. The debate Davis's book opened is summarized, with key articles reprinted, in Thomas Bender, ed., *The Antislavery Debate: Capitalism and Abolitionism As a Problem in Historical Interpretation* (Berkeley: University of California Press, 1992).

INDEX